Chris Rowe knows the Xs and Os of the golf swing, but he possesses something more rare: An understanding of how the game is played and the travails of the everyday player. Through funny, poignant firsthand anecdotes, he conveys a wisdom that will help you play better and enjoy the game more.

—Guy Yocom
Golf Digest

This book is fresh and inspiring. Chris Rowe has a way of drawing us all into the story. His story is our story. ... It is the story of the brotherhood of this great chase. Read, enjoy, reflect, and then go chase par once again. This is a great read!

—Dr. David Cook
Author of *Golf's Sacred Journey*

The best golf coaches, the Harvey Penicks and Tommy Armours, engage their pupils in a sort of Socratic dialogue, that being the proven path to true understanding and subsequent improvement. Chris Rowe, aka the Wizard of Whispering Pines, is a master at this type of instruction. Chris also has a gift for anecdotal teaching, the proof being this delightful collection of Penick-style ruminations on golf, golfers, and our never-ending search for The Secret. If you haven't read Rowe, you're making the game harder than it needs to be.

—John Garrity
Sports Illustrated writer and author of *Tiger 2.0: The Best of John Garrity* and *Ancestral Links: A Golf Obsession Spanning Generations*

He Who Looks Up Shall See a Bad Shot

Chris Rowe

First published by Dog Ear Publishing
4010 W. 86th Street, Ste H
Indianapolis, IN 46268
www.dogearpublishing.net

ISBN: 978-1-4575-2556-8

This book is printed on acid-free paper.

Printed in the United States of America

To my beautiful wife, Tamara. You are my biggest fan and encourager! You have always been there for me in the best and worst of times. God truly blessed me more than I ever deserved when you said yes at the stroke of midnight 2000 with fireworks lighting up the Fort Worth sky-line.

To Dylan, Pierce, and Jude, the best sons I could have ever asked for. Each one of you has your own special talents and will do great things.

To my mom and dad for all your support and for always believing in me!

To God for giving me the passion and desire to make a difference in the game of golf and in the lives of all the wonderful people I come in con-tact with every day.

A Call from the Misses

Playing golf with my dad and father-in-law is always a treat. They were both in town for my son's kindergarten graduation, and we had to sneak some golf in before they returned home. They both arrived at the club early to warm up, and then we were off to the first tee. The tee box had a group, and there was a group in the first fairway. I've never made a double eagle, but going to the third tee instead of playing behind two groups all day was as close as I have come to that amazing feat.

We teed off on three with incredible weather and proceeded to have a great time. When we putted out on the eighteenth green, I asked my dad if he wanted to play the first two holes to finish our round. He said he would, so we drove over to the first tee for the second time that day. After we played the first hole, we teed off on our last hole of the day, the par-five second. This hole is a big boy's hole with bunkers everywhere, length, and a difficult green. My tee shot was hit okay, but nothing spectacular. The ball cleared the top of the hill and rolled down to 220 yard marker from the green. My next shot required a carry of 215 yards, over a massive bunker, with very little room for error. I hit a three iron a little bit on the heel of the club and really didn't think it would carry, but somehow, it just cleared the bunker and stopped twelve feet from the hole. Now here is where the story becomes interesting.

My wife called after my second shot and needed to ask me a question. All of us have had calls on the golf course that we should not take, and cell phones, in my opinion, should never be allowed on a golf course, even though I am guilty of this and always have mine with me. I answered and found out that the family wanted to go see the new Pixar movie. The movie started at 4:50 and would be impossible for me to be able to attend, but the next movie didn't start until 7:50, and that would be too late for the kids. I love Pixar movies and really wanted to see this movie, so I suggested going on Saturday. That was not going to work because the kids had been promised months before that they would see this movie on opening day, and they had their hearts set on going. This created a marital spat on my last hole of the day with a twelve-foot eagle putt hanging in the balance. I don't make a lot of eagles, and this would be only my second eagle on this hole in my life. The eagle putt was important, but so was the movie. My wife was telling me every reason why they should go to the 4:50 showing, and my dad and father-in-law had already made their putts. As my dad and father-in-law looked at me, wondering why in the world I had answered the phone, I realized the eagle putt didn't matter that much because the phone conversation had driven me to a point of utter craziness. Instead of looking at the line of the putt, instead of taking a practice stroke, instead of caring the least bit, I held the phone down near my waist in my left hand and took a one-handed stroke at the ball. The ball rolled right into the cup for eagle while my wife was still talking to me about the movie. I smiled at my dad, put the phone next to my ear, and said, "Just go to the 4:50 movie."

Here is the moral to this story: Not one shot out of the three was great. My drive was just okay, my second shot was lucky, and my one-handed putt didn't matter to me. So many times, we get perfectionist attitudes toward golf. None of us will ever conquer this game, but we will all continue to try to hold on to the rare moments when the game is nice to us. Golf is a game of misses. Where we miss our shots determines what we shoot. No one ever asks, "How great did you hit the ball?" They ask, "What did you shoot?" You can look at my eagle on this day in many ways, but you can bet I will not answer my phone the next time I have an eagle putt, because I could never be that lucky again!

A Chili Cheeseburger and a Conversation

A few days ago, I was playing with some of our members on a Saturday morning. My game was so off, it was scary. My driver couldn't find a fairway, my putting was horrible, and I was not having much fun. When we made the turn, there were a few groups on the tenth hole, so we decided to have lunch. Byron Stillwell and I had lunch while Dan Spain went to the range to work on his game. Byron ordered a chili cheeseburger, and we talked about antacids, age, life, and friendships. Golf was not on either one of our minds during this time, but we were going to have to face the course again after we finished our meal whether we liked it or not. We decided to tee off on the front nine and play the first and second hole and then go over to the tenth tee to finish our round. The first tee shot after lunch started out much like the tee shots earlier in the day. They were not going where I wanted them to go, and scrambling was becoming a way of life on this day. I managed to make a par and made my way to the second hole. At this point, I was wishing I was anywhere but on a golf course. On the second hole, I hit a decent tee shot, hit a decent lay-up on this par five and then hit a gap wedge very close for a birdie. We then made our way to the back nine to finish our round. My tee shot on the tenth tee was basically a worm burner down the middle. I had 154 yards to the hole and hit an eight iron to about ten feet. I missed the putt but felt a little better about the round. On the eleventh hole, I hit a decent tee shot and then hit a horrible six iron to the wrong side of an extremely difficult green. I had to make a choice whether to putt or chip off a very tight lie to a pin that had a double break. I decided to putt the ball. It rolled four feet to the left, started to break to the right, and then started to straighten at the hole. To my surprise, the putt dropped for a birdie. I could have hit the putt a thousand times and never made it again. It was pure luck!

Now my mindset started to change, and I started to feel like the back nine could be good. I missed a good birdie chance on twelve but birdied the thirteenth. On the fourteenth, I hit a great drive and had sand wedge to a tightly tucked pin. The shot was okay, but not close enough to guarantee birdie. I made par on fifteen and came to the sixteenth hole needing to make a birdie to win money in the birdie game we were playing that day. The hole was playing 186 yards with a crosswind from left to right. I grabbed a five iron and took dead aim at the flag. The ball had a gentle fade and landed six feet below the hole. I studied the putt and made a good stroke to watch the ball disappear into the bottom of the cup. The seventeenth is a great par five that is usually a birdie hole. The wind was blowing pretty good from left to right, and even though I was four under in my last nine holes, I was not confident in the shot. I decided to play a fade off the left fairway bunkers. The shot came off perfectly but went too far and landed in the bunker. After trying to play safe, I hit the ball behind a tree and made a stupid bogey. Three under the last ten holes with the hardest hole in Texas left to play.

The tee shot on the eighteenth at Whispering Pines Golf Club is unbelievably demanding, with a long carry over water, bunkers down the left side, and hazard to the right. I hit my tee shot as well as I could possibly hit a ball. I was left with 138 yards to a flag placed on the front of the green with a severe false front. If the ball were hit three feet short of the flag, it would roll back in the water. I was stuck between a soft eight iron or a hard nine iron. I chose nine and made a perfect swing, with the ball landing five feet past the cup. I now had a birdie putt to shoot four under in the last eleven holes. The putt, unfortunately, just missed, but I had just shot thirty-four on the back nine and one under for the two warm-up holes.

This game is, without a doubt, the craziest of all sports. One minute, I am ready to quit, and the next minute, my game completely turns around. The moral to this story is that a chili cheeseburger and a conversation might not make you play great, but the break in the action might be much needed. It got my mind off golf for a little while. You never know when a putt might drop or you might catch a lucky break. The next time you are having the worst round of your life, stop at the turn and get a chili cheeseburger and see if it has the same effect on your game as it did with mine. Oh, and by the way, don't forget the antacids.

A Conversation with Paula Creamer's Father

Paula Creamer was the captain for Team USA at the 2009 Spirit International at Whispering Pines. It is a rare opportunity to be able to speak to a parent of a child who has achieved a successful career in a professional sport. The opportunity was there for me for an entire week, and the conversation started as a simple question on the driving range: What advice would you give a parent of a child who wants to play professional golf? The next forty-five minutes were filled with an incredible story of a father's love for his daughter and of the sacrifice of a family to help their daughter achieve her dream.

Mr. Creamer loved golf, but Paula didn't show much interest in the game at an early age. Mr. Creamer never pushed her to play but hoped she would someday fall in love with the game the way he had. One day, she asked him if she could go to the driving range with him. He told me that he had been stunned because she had never asked to go before. Paula went to the range with her dad, hit a couple of balls, and went to the snack shack and got a candy bar. The next time Mr. Creamer went to the range, Paula once again asked if she could go. That time, she hit a few more balls, but the golf bug had not taken hold just yet. After they had repeated this process for a while, Mr. Creamer suggested that Paula might take a lesson from one of the golf professionals at their club. Mr. Creamer told Paula she could pick any of the pros to give the lesson and the choice was totally up to her. Here is the funny part of the story.

Mr. Creamer really wanted Paula to pick one particular pro, but he would not suggest it or try to sway her decision. Paula thought about this and made her decision. I don't remember the professional's name, but Mr. Creamer referred to him as the fourth assistant to the assistant. Basically, this guy was as far down the chain of command as you could get. Mr. Creamer once again honored his word and bought a series of lesson from this pro.

The lessons were to begin, but not before Mr. Creamer and the young pro had a talk about how to teach Paula. Mr. Creamer told the pro that he was going to tell him something that the pro would probably never hear from a parent. Here were his instructions: "This is my one opportunity for my daughter to fall in love with golf, and she has chosen you to be her instructor. Make every lesson fun! If you want to drive around and never hit a golf ball and just watch people on the course playing, you can. Just make it fun!" Mr. Creamer didn't care how good Paula became; he just wanted her to love the game.

As Paula progressed rapidly, her dad knew she had a special talent. Paula started to dominate at every 1 level when she had to make a life-changing decision at a very young age. Paula was a cheerleader. Imagine that! The problem was that cheerleading was going to conflict with her golf schedule. It would be impossible for her to do both. Cheerleading was what the popular girls did, and she was going to isolate herself from her friends if she gave it up. Paula went to her dad and asked his opinion. Mr. Creamer always made her choicesit about his daughter and asked her, "Paula, do you want to cheer for people, or do you want people to cheer for you?" That might be the greatest parent-to-child line ever given! We all know what decision she made, and wow, do people ever cheer for her!

Paula's parents made many sacrifices for their daughter. They moved from California to Florida so she could attend the David Leadbetter Academy. They invested in her future, and now she is a superstar on the LPGA Tour, but the greatest thing her parents did was show her love. Mr. Creamer's story was incredible to listen to. Many parents could take notes from it on how to be great parents as well as how to help their children achieve their own dreams.

Being a golf professional for eighteen years, I have seen many parents who wanted their children to achieve their—the parents'—dreams, not the children's own dreams. I have seen many children whose parents told me they had the next Tiger Woods and wanted me to help get their children on the PGA Tour. All of these parents had good intentions, but most of the time, the kids burned out or were just playing because their parents wanted them to. All of you reading this know that I believe golf is the greatest of all sports, not because it is my profession, but for all the great people you meet along the way. If your kids have potential, let them have fun first and develop second. If they can get their educations paid for, that's a bonus. The professional dreams can come after the scholarship. The Paula Creamers of the world are a rarity, but being great parents and building our relationships with our children shouldn't be rarities.

The Wolf Game

The other day, I was visiting my family in Fort Worth for July Fourth weekend. We watched fireworks, cooked out, and had a lot of great family time. No trip to Fort Worth is complete without eating Railhead BBQ, Uncle Julio's and going by Colonial to play golf with your buddies in a wolf game.

For those of you reading this who have never played wolf, let me explain. Your group tees off in alphabetical order, and the person who tees off first each time is the wolf. The wolf can pick a player after he hits his tee shot to be his partner, but he has to make the decision before the next person tees off. There is definitely some strategy involved in this game. One of the very interesting strategies is going lone wolf. This happens when the player decides he doesn't want to pick anyone and plays against the entire group by himself. This also doubles the bet! This only happens a few times during a round, and it seems to happen every time I play with one particular individual.

The individual's name is Rob Hood. Doesn't that sound like the name of a guy who shoots arrows and takes money from the rich? Well, I am not rich, but this guy seems to take money from all of us when we get to the fifteenth hole at Colonial. I am still not sure how he does it, but he is always the wolf on this hole based on the alphabetical order that was decided on the first hole. I secretly think he doesn't invite people who will screw up the order so he will always have the fifteenth hole. (Just kidding!)

The game started, and the money started changing hands as we make our way through the historic links. None of us hit it like Ben Hogan, but we were having a good time. Rob struggled for the majority of the day. On the eighth hole, I offered a swing tip, which he declined. On the twelfth, he accepted the tip and hit the ball in the Trinity River. We got to the fifteenth hole, and somehow, it was miraculously his turn to be the wolf. He hit a good drive down the middle, but nothing extraordinary. I was next and hit my best drive of the entire day, only needing a wedge to reach this tough par four. Rob passed on taking me as his partner and then passed on everyone else in the group. He called out, *"Lone wolf!"* This wasn't the first time he had done this, and I already knew pretty much what to expect. I hit my wedge about twelve feet below the cup, and he hit a mid iron to the front right portion of the green. Everyone else was pretty much out of the hole, and Rob was getting a shot based on his handicap. He putted the ball, and it came up three feet short; I missed mine just barely on the left side of the hole and tapped in for par. Rob lined up his putt and rammed it into the back of the cup for a four net three and another victory.

Golfers always have holes that fit their shot patterns or play into their strengths. Some of you reading this might say the handicap on the hole played into his hands. Well, that is not the case, because I have seen him birdie with no strokes before. The key to this story is that Rob has confidence in his ability to play the fifteenth hole. He had a difficult day for seventeen holes but played very well on one hole. As golfers, our mindsets change when we come to holes we have played well in the past. We draw upon past success and are able to perform well no matter how much pressure we might feel. The best way to achieve this is to start remembering all the good shots you have hit rather than dwelling on the bad ones. You seldom hear the great players talk about their bad shots; rather, they talk about the good shots.

We all have selective memories and can choose what we want to think about. Next time you play that hole that gives you trouble, try to remember a great tee shot you have hit in the past. When you get to your next shot, try to think of a great iron shot you have hit that is similar to the shot you currently have. Continue this process for each shot until you hole out. If you try this, I bet you'll play more holes like Rob Hood plays the fifteenth at Colonial.

Advice to the Fallen Tour Player

This week, I took some of my members to Augusta to watch the Masters. The beauty of the golf course is indescribable. It is one of the few places I have been that actually lives up to the hype. After I had eaten a pimento cheese sandwich, bought merchandise for the wife and kids, and taken pictures, a thought came to me about this crazy game. I saw many players whom we don't see anymore on the PGA Tour who have won the Masters and are invited back each year despite the condition of their games. If you watch golf telecasts today, all you see is Tiger, whether he is playing well or badly. If he decides not to play, you probably don't watch. Can you imagine if Tiger lost his game and became a David Duval or Ian Baker Finch? We don't think something like that could ever happen, but look down the list of incredible players who can't play at the competitive level they used to. David Duval was the number-one player in the world, and we all know what has happened with his game. Chip Beck was a Ryder Cup hero and shot fifty-nine in the Las Vegas Invitational but has fallen off the PGA Tour. Watch a Nationwide Tour event sometime and see how many once-great players are now playing on that tour. The list is long, and none of these players ever thought they would struggle the way they have with their games, but they have.

The point is that this game is unbelievably difficult and humbling. On the days we play great, the game seems easy, and on the days we struggle, it seems overwhelmingly hard. I watched Seve, my childhood hero, hit incredible shots that wowed the crowd, and he still had the charisma that made him a superstar. His golf game hasn't had a pulse since he won the 1988 British Open. After watching him play his practice round, I thought he might make the cut. That thought went out the window when he posted eighty-six on Thursday. How can these guys fall so far from the top? I think it starts as a mental issue and then becomes physical. Seve has commented that he was never the same after the missed putt in the playoff with Larry Mize and Greg Norman in the 1987 Masters. Self-doubt along with swing issues can cause the greatest of players to fall off the pinnacles they once stood on.

Another problem that seems to plague many players is the desire to change their games and take it to the next level. How much higher can you go after winning one of the fourmajors? How many tour guys go from teacher to teacher, trying to find the missing link to achieve more distance or to perfect their swings? These players are always looking and searching for the edge when they should stick with what has gotten them to where they are. If you are good enough to get on tour, you are pretty darn good. The PGA Tour doesn't just hand out cards to anyone; you have to earn it. If you are good enough to win a major, then you are in a totally different category altogether. My advice to any tour player who reads this article is that there is only one Tiger and it is not his swing that has won all the tournaments. It is his mind and his short game.

Here is my advice to the fallen tour player: Go work on your short game twice as long as you work on your swing. I tell my students that for every ball they hit on the range, they should hit two putts and two chips. Write down your goals and change your attitude. Think like a champion, and you can become one. I don't have all the answers, and if I did, I would be on the tour instead of teaching golf, selling merchandise, and running a club. I am the most blessed golf professional in the country, but the reality is, all club professionals wish they were inside the ropes at Augusta, playing, and all the tour players who are playing the Nationwide Tour or commentating on television wish they were playing at Augusta too.

Anxiety at Pebble Beach

Every year, I take three members to the Mizuno Pro Am in Pebble Beach, California. This tournament is played on Spyglass Hill, Spanish Bay, and Pebble Beach. I have been taking members to this tournament for ten years, and I can usually tell you within a shot what my score will be at each course. This event is somewhat like a major to all the pros who participate. You are playing incredible courses, teams come from all over the country, and it is played the day after the AT&T. The scoreboards are still up, and you might even see a few celebrities around the hotel. All of these distractions make you want to play your best golf.

Over the years, I would practice very hard, take at least one lesson, and stress out about how I would play once we arrived on the Monterrey Peninsula. This never worked, and it only frustrated me more that I had worked harder than normal for a special event and then not play up to my standards. One day, I was in Fort Worth, taking a lesson from my instructor, and asked him how to prepare for this event. He told me I had two options. Option one: play a lot of tournaments. Option two: quit caring about playing great. Option one was not going to be an option because of family time and teaching. Option two was my new route to go. This did not mean I took a John Daly approach to golf but that I changed my attitude of what people might think if my score wasn't low. What I came to realize is that people don't care nearly as much about what you shoot as they do about the friendships and laughs they have with you on the course. Life is too short to be overly concerned about a score! Think about how much better fathers or friends we could be if we put as much time and commitment into those relationships as we do into preparing for golf tournaments.

The tournament was to start on a Wednesday, but we were playing Cypress Point on Tuesday morning. If you ever want to play well, this is the place to do it. We teed off in very cold temperatures, and then the rains came, followed by sleet on the ninth. They were extremely difficult playing conditions, but I hit the ball fantastically. The next morning was the moment of truth. The tournament coordinators were on the tee, announcing our names. Here was my chance to see how this new attitude would work! I teed up my ball and felt an unusual calm about the day. In the past, I had been extremely nervous and hit some pretty wild tee shots. This tee shot, though, ripped down the center, and a birdie followed. I was off to the races with this new attitude. The end result was a good score on a very difficult Spyglass golf course.

The rest of the trip went just as the first tee shot at Spyglass had. My scoring average was much lower than it had ever been, and this tournament was suddenly fun. Sure, I hit some bad shots during the week, but I did not let them change my attitude. Remember, the only thing you can control on the golf course is you!

When we arrived back in Houston, my members mentioned how well I had played. This was nice to hear and really solidified the idea that how you think about yourself and your golf game really effects your score. If you stress out about hitting a golf ball, you are going to be miserable. If you try your best and win or don't win, your attitude shouldn't change. Try this the next time you are preparing for a tournament, and see if your scores don't improve.

Blackjack and Golf Swings

Many of you have been to Las Vegas and played blackjack. The object of the game is to try to beat the dealer by getting to twenty-one without going over or having the dealer go over twenty-one. Many of us have sat at a blackjack table for many hours with success at times, but most of the time, not so much. A friend of mine who frequents Vegas numerous times a year told me a very important piece of advice when gambling: *If you lose three hands in a row, walk away.* This does not mean you walk away from the game forever; it means you leave the area and find another game or another blackjack table. By walking away, you give your mind time to clear. You have the opportunity to take a much-needed break, and when your luck goes south, you need a change.

Many times on the driving range, I see this same type of issue with the golfers. You can leave a student after his lesson and give him a detailed idea of what he or she should work on for the next week. You start your next lesson and happen to notice that your previous student is slashing away at range balls at light speed. This happens all the time on driving ranges across the country. When students get frustrated, they change their tempos and start hitting balls as fast as they can to try to correct a swing that was there only a few minutes before. The person who makes his practice sessions like this is the same as the guy who sits at the blackjack table for hours, thinking his luck is going to change. Both student and gambler unfortunately end up in the same situation: physically broken in the swing and broke in the wallet. The moral to this story is that when things start going bad, you should walk away. The golf balls are not going anywhere, and there will be another blackjack table around the corner. Those casinos are still being built, and the money building them is from the people who don't get up and walk away. Next time you are on the range and you start hitting poor shots, step away, get a drink, or talk to someone on the range, but do not keep hacking away. Just stepping away for a few minutes can make all the difference.

Break up Your Round

A few weeks ago, I was on the putting green with a student and asked him to make ten putts in a row from six feet. My student would make six and then miss. Then he would make eight in a row and then miss the ninth. This process continued for about fifteen minutes. There was nothing wrong with his stroke, but the closer he came to reaching his goal, the more the putts quit dropping. My student was placing more emphasis on the final putts even though every putt counted exactly the same. The funniest comment I hear golf commentators make when describing shots on television is "This is the most important shot of the tournament." This is the furthest thing from the truth. Every shot in a round of golf counts as one shot! No shot is more important than another.

Let's get back to my student on the putting green. After watching my student putt and continue to miss every time he started getting close to the magic number, I made a suggestion. I told him to make three putts in a row. After he did that, we talked about something besides golf. I then told him to make four putts in a row. After he did that, we talked about something besides golf. I then asked him to make three in a row, and he did. I looked at my student and told him he had just made ten putts in a row and accomplished the goal. He didn't really realize what he had done, because we had broken up the drill into three drills. We made each task seem easier, when, in reality, there was no difference. Once I got the student focused on a smaller task that he felt he could accomplish, he made putts. Once he quit thinking about making ten in a row and instead focused on making three or four in a row, he was able to make ten in row and achieve the goal.

When you are on the golf course, try to break up your round into six rounds of three holes. Instead of trying to shoot a nine-hole or eighteen-hole score, focus on fewer stretches of holes. This will keep your mind from getting too far ahead in the round. Every shot is just as important as the next, but tricking yourself into playing three-hole rounds will keep you from making mistakes toward the end of the round!

Changes Are Tough to Make

Have you ever taken a lesson and the pro told you he was going to rebuild your swing? The phrase "rebuild your swing" has become very popular among teachers. My belief is that your golf swing will have many of the same characteristics, regardless of how many lessons you take. A good teacher will evaluate the swing and make recommendations to correct the flaws that consistently plague your game.

Take Tiger Woods, who has hit more golf balls than you or I ever will but still lowers his head and body at impact. Do you not think he hasn't tried to correct this swing flaw? This move is part of his swing that he has had since he started swinging a golf club. It is almost like trying to change someone's personality. You can work on changing your personality, but you will always have many of those characteristics that have been passed down through your family genetics. Tiger has made some changes since he started working with Hank Haney, but does his swing really look that different from when he was working with Butch Harmon? The average golfer might not see the changes Tiger has made, I believe he still would have won the British Open with or without the swing changes. Tiger was in total control of his game then, just like five years ago at St. Andrews. The Masters, in contrast, was pure Tiger gutting out and fighting his swing all the way around the National and still finding a way to win. His swing that week was not the same swing that we saw at the British last year. It was definitely better, and the changes are starting to become engrained. Is Tiger's swing better today than it was in 2000? That is not for me to judge, but they are both pretty darn good, whether you are a Hank fan or a Butch fan. The point I am trying to make after all of the Tiger talk is that making changes in your golf swing takes some time before you start to feel comfortable. Most changes you make in your life or in your golf swing take weeks, sometimes even months, to take effect. The key to making changes is to keep working until they become engrained, to know your flaws, and to continue to have regular maintenance with your instructor.

Could You Beat Tiger Woods in a Putting Contest?

Probably not, but you would have a chance. Unlike on the golf course, where nobody has a chance to beat a healthy Tiger, on the putting green, it can be a different story. Think about it. There is nothing physical to putting. You would never have to hit a mammoth drive. You would never have to hit a shot over water or out of a bunker. You would just have to out-putt him on a typical putting green. So how could you beat him?

First, you would need to have a great routine in which you can make every putt seem just like another putt. Let's compare "the win for the ages" putt in the 1997 Masters with the 2000 PGA putt to tie Bob May on the seventy-second hole to force a playoff. If you could watch both putts on television side by side, you would notice the routines were exactly the same. Both putts were of similar distance, but one was with a huge lead and the other was to tie just to have a chance to play extra holes. In the 1997 Masters, he could have putt with only one hand and with his eyes closed and still won the tournament. In the 2000 PGA, it was a must-make. When you see the replays, you see that he treated each putt the same.

Second, you would need to have a couple of warm-up matches to get your nerves under control. Just being in the presence of the greatest golfer of our time would be intimidating.

Third, you would need to have light grip pressure while keeping your head steady through impact. Count to two before you look, and stay in your posture. The biggest problem I see with my students is standing up right after impact. One of the most famous putts of all time was probably Justin Leonard's putt to win the Ryder Cup. If you watch Justin, you'll see that after hitting that putt, he stayed in his posture until the ball was just a few feet from the cup. That putt was a very long putt, and he never stood up but stayed over the ball with just his head turned toward the hole.

Try these three tips for great putting. You probably will never have the chance to challenge Tiger on the putting green, but it is without question the only part of the game any of us would have a chance to beat him in.

Cut off the Fat in Your Swing

Have you ever had a steak that had a big chunk of fat on it? If you were at a nice restaurant, you probably would send the steak back to the kitchen. If you were at home, you would probably cut the fat off and eat only the meat. Rib eye steaks will be excluded in this article.

I use this illustration at least once a week when I'm teaching a student about shortening his or her swing. When the backswing becomes too long, numerous things can happen, and the majority of the time, those things are not good! I honestly can't count the number of times I've asked students to make a backswing and stop just past their pockets and I've then shown them on video where they actually stopped. What we feel and what is real are never the same in golf swings. Almost every time, the students can't believe what they are seeing on video. Their backswings stops very close to parallel when they feel like they went only halfway back. I call this cutting off the fat in the golf swing. Fat is no good on your body or in your golf swing! When you take out the twenty percent extra that is not needed in the swing, you get all meat. When you don't have the access, you don't have to compensate as much to make the downswing.

The next time you go out to the range, try to make a half swing and have someone film you with a phone. I will bet you will be surprised at where you actually stop your club.

The next time you order a steak and there is big chunk of fat, remember this golf lesson, but don't complain to the chef if your significant other cooked it.

Derek Jeter, Tiger Woods, and a Gray Hair

My age is slowly, but surely, starting to catch up with me. As I was getting ready for work the other day, I noticed a gray hair. I took a pair of tweezers and started the process of trying to extract the hair from my thinning scalp. After missing on several attempts, I noticed that looking in the mirror to try to perform a task is very difficult. When trying to maneuver a pair of tweezers while looking in a mirror, you have to do everything opposite of what it looks like. When I thought my hand was moving toward my target (gray hair), it was actually moving away. When I thought my hand was moving away from my target, it was actually moving toward my target. After several minutes of trying to pluck a hair from my head, I came to another one of my golf epiphanies. This got me thinking about watching Tiger Woods make practice swings. When Tiger takes his practice swing, he swings across the intended line of his swing. When Derek Jeter takes his practice swings before stepping up to home plate, he swings exaggeratedly downward. Each of these superstars makes his practice swings the opposite of what he is trying to do in his real swing.

The most common swing mistake for PGA Tour players is getting the club stuck too far behind their bodies on their downswings. The worst swing an MLB player can make is to swing up on the ball, causing a pop-up. The next time you watch television and either sport is being played, watch how the players make their practice swings. You will notice they all make the swings exactly as I have described. Now, all you golfers reading this, don't go out and start trying to make your practice swings like Tiger's, because the majority of you are already doing this in your real golf swings. You should actually try to do just the opposite of Tiger and try to swing as far to the right as you can.

The moral to this story is that the best way to groove your swing is to sometimes practice just the opposite of your swing flaw. If your golf shots always start to the left and slice back, then you should try to make practice swings as far right as you can and release your hands. If you hit shots that start way right and hook back, use Tiger's method of making

18

practice swings with a cut across path and hold the face open. This might sound technical, but what you feel in your swing is almost always the opposite of what really happens. Try these practice swing drills the next time you play, and if any of you have a solution for eliminating gray hair, will you let me know?

Did Your Golf Swing Get Quick?

Fat shots and thin shots have one thing in common. Both swings were rushed on the downswing. A fat shot happens when a golfer lowers his right side and hits behind the ball. A thin shot happens when a golfer straightens his body at impact. Neither one of these shots produces great results, but both happen when the player gets quick on his or her downswing. The next time you are on the range and you are hitting thin or fat shots, try to slow your tempo. Think of making a swing on a tempo count of one, two, and three. Say these words as you make your swing. Takeaway is one, downswing is two, and impact is three. Some tour players even think of a word in their minds at the top of their backswings to slow the transition. The key for controlling the transition from backswing to downswing is to control the tempo. A player can swing as hard as he wants as long as the tempo count has a consistent rhythm. Nick Price has a very quick swing and Fred Couples has a very smooth swing, but they both keep a consistent swing count, meaning the rhythm of the swings is spaced out and not rushed. Try slowing your tempo and see if it doesn't help you hit better shots.

Dinner with Bob Rotella

Recently, I had the opportunity to have dinner with Dr. Bob Rotella, who has always been a huge fan of mine. Spending time with him was truly an honor. Dr. Bob was with Padrig Harrington the entire week of the British Open, and, as many of you know, Padrig double-bogeyed the last hole in regulation. The doc told us he was trying to think of what to say to his student after Harrington had possibly blown the opportunity to win the British Open. These were his words as soon as Padrig walked off the green: "That was the best up and down I have ever seen." Wow, Padrig looked like he had lost the Open, but he and his mental coach were still being positive about the situation. Well, as we all know, after the press conference, Sergio sounded like the guy who gets every bad break and Padrig was holding the Claret Jug.

After he spoke about the British Open, he talked about Tiger and how great a mind he has. This is no revelation to anyone reading this, but Rotella did say there are plenty of people who have the talent that Tiger has but none have Tiger's mind. He said, "Isn't it funny that the two best players in the world hit it the most crooked." This is a true statement, and if you watch Tiger and Phil, you'll see they are constantly in the woods but are magicians around the greens. Their minds and their belief in their touch around the greens keep them in tournaments.

When dessert came, I asked Dr. Bob a question about my childhood hero, Seve Ballesteros. I asked him if he could help a guy like Seve, and to my surprise, he told me that Seve had come to talk to him years ago. Seve was the perfect example of a wonderful feel player who became caught up in mechanics. Between Mac O'Grady and David Leadbetter, Seve lost his way on the golf course. The doc said the guys on tour were happy to see Seve retire because it was tough to watch such a great champion struggle the way he had.

The last thing the doc discussed was acceptance of every shot. He said it doesn't matter what happened on your last shot, be it good or bad;

just accept it and move on. The game beats you up enough, so why beat yourself up?

When the evening ended, I felt like I had just had a mental turn-around. It is hard to stay positive in this crazy game, but the reality is, we can control only one thing, and that is our attitude. There were many other stories told, but these are the ones that stood out the most. Next time you tee it up, accept each shot regardless of the outcome, work on your short game more, and stay positive like Padrig Harrington. You might not win the British Open, but you will probably play better than before.

Get Rid of the Infection in Your Golf Swing

All of you reading this have gone to the doctor at one time or another to treat an infection. I tend to get sinus infections in the spring and fall because of the pollen and mountain cedar in east Texas. My eyes itch, my throat hurts, my body aches, and I have many other symptoms we can all relate to. When I go to my doctor, he doesn't provide a different prescription for each symptom. He usually gives me an antibiotic to kill the infection, which takes care of all the other symptoms in my body.

When giving a golf lesson, I like to take the same approach. I believe everyone has some type of infection in his golf swing and the infection causes many of the other symptoms. Take for example a person who slices the ball by lifting the club on his takeaway and comes over the swing plane on his downswing while using no lower body. I could have the student rotate his hips faster or drop the club to the inside or turn his hands over at impact. Many of these suggestions could help the student for a while, but all of these suggestions are Band-Aids for an infection. To cure all of these symptoms, the student could make a full shoulder turn, which would allow him to start his downswing on plane as well as rotate through impact without having to manipulate the club. By making a full shoulder turn, the infection will start to leave the golf swing and the symptoms will do the same. This is only one example of many that I could talk about, but you get the point. You don't treat a sinus infection with Advil. Advil will help, but it will not get rid of the infection.

The prescription from your golf professional has the same instructions your pharmacist gives you when you receive your medicine: Take all of your prescription until gone. This means do not work on this for two days and then go on to some band-aid that will land you back in the golf emergency room. Take that lesson you have been putting off and do what the golf doctor tells you. If you get rid of your infection, you will feel better and play better.

Giant Arms & Small Legs

How many times have you seen a guy coming out of the gym or walking around the grocery store wearing a super-tight shirt to show off his muscles? Not to get weird, but how many of those guys had huge upper bodies and small lower bodies? This made me think of how out of proportion their bodies look. They don't work enough on their lower bodies to match the upper bodies. In golf, this happens with short game and long game. Most of you spend all of your practice time beating balls on the range. If you are honest, you'll admit that the percentage of range versus short-game practice is way out of proportion.

When I worked at Colonial, I always marveled at the touring professional practice sessions. The person who impressed me the most was Nick Faldo. Sir Nick showed up early Thursday morning with a late-morning tee time. He was one of the first pros to get to the range that morning and started his practice session of going through the entire bag. After he hit balls for about an hour, he went to the short-game area, where he spent another hour chipping, pitching, putting, and hitting bunker shots. He then went to the first tee and played his round. Sir Nick was a six-time major champion. He wasn't the dominant player at this time in his career, but he still had a balanced practice routine. After he posted his score and ate lunch, he repeated the entire practice session before leaving the grounds. All of you aspiring golfers who would like to play on the PGA Tour, follow this model!

The point to this story is of a balanced approach to practice. If you're an incredible ball striker but can't get the ball up and down when you miss a green, you look like the big-arms-and-small-legs guy. Spend an equal amount of time in all areas of your game. Obviously, there will be days when you need to spend more time on certain parts of your game where you are struggling, but don't neglect the other areas. Tiger Woods is a great example of this. A few years ago when he started working with Sean Foley, he spent so much time working on his ball striking that his putting suffered. Now he has rectified this and has balanced out his game with the statistics to back it up.

If you do go to the gym, work all areas of your body so you don't look like that guy. In your golf game, take the balanced approach to your practice sessions and you will see the results on the course!

Golf Swing Warning Lights

Isn't it the worst feeling when you get in your car and one of the warning lights comes on? Your car is telling you something is wrong, and you have to deal with it whether you want to or not. Sometimes it is not a big deal, like your windshield wiper fluid being low, but sometimes it is the check engine light, which demands immediate attention.

When we play golf, we have these lights come on all the time, but we seldom pay attention like we would if a warning light came on in our cars. If you have a light in your golf swing that says it needs service, you should see your golf instructor immediately If your golf-swing light says fluid levels low, you might need to look at your setup or your grip. If it's the temperature gauge that's lit up, you might need to check your attitude and put golf into perspective. If the gas gauge is on empty, you might need to evaluate your health and look at your workout schedule and diet.

All of us have these lights in our golf swings. If you go too long with a light on in your swing, you will eventual run into major swing repairs. Watch your ball flight along with divots to gauge what your swing path is doing. Check your setup, alignment, and posture before each shot. All of these are lights to pay attention to. You take your car in every 3,000 miles for an oil change, but do you see your golf instructor at least once a month? We take our warning lights seriously in our cars but neglect our golf swings too often. I encourage each of you reading this article to write down your warning lights for your golf swing, pay attention to them, and get regular maintenance on your swing. When we take these precautions, our golf swings run like well-oiled machines. When we neglect them, we have major repair bills to get us running again. So go see your golf mechanic and get all your lights checked out this week!

Golf Swings and Personalities

M any people have similar personalities, but no two personalities are just alike. Every kid around the world today tries to copy Tiger Woods's swing, but on the PGA Tour, how many people have even a similar swing to Tiger's? Adam Scott is probably the only person who comes close. Jack Nicklaus, the greatest player of all time, had only one person who came close to his swing, and that was Tom Weiskoff. How about Lee Trevino and Ben Hogan, two of the greatest ball strikers to ever play the game? I can't think of anyone who swung like Trevino. Hogan has probably had more written about him than any player living or deceased, and you don't see anyone today or from thirty years ago who swings exactly like him. No one has a swing just like yours, so accept your swing and continue to try to make it better.

In the golf business, you see a lot of swings; they are all different. I can look down the tenth fairway at Whispering Pines Golf Club and tell you exactly which member just hit their shot. We all have our mannerisms that we wish we could get rid of. Someone might see your swing and say, "I wish my swing looked like his." On the other hand, while that person is admiring your swing, you might hate your swing and wish you could change it.

The key to your swing is acceptance of what the good Lord gave you. Find a teacher who can identify what you need to work on, and spend the rest of your life working on those things. If you knew what to work on for the rest of your life, you wouldn't waste time changing your swing every time a new swing theory came out in *Golf Digest*. There is no new information in teaching; it is all old information that some other teacher told his student years ago. Stack and tilt, for instance, is one of the new teaching theories, but Mac O'Grady was teaching the same theories back in the eighties.

You can't change your personality, either, but you can work on the way you act and treat people. We can make changes in our golf swings with the help of good golf instructors. You can make changes in your personality after constructive criticism from a mentor or a spouse or from life lessons. Your personality and your golf swing will always have characteristics that you were born with. Here is a great rule of thumb for life and golf: Treat people the way you would like to be treated; the journey is the reward; work on your game like Tiger does, and you will probably be successful in both.

Good Days and Bad Days

Why is it you can play a great round of golf one day and the very next day play like you have never played before? The reason lies in the fact that we play an extremely difficult game. Consistency in golf is probably harder than in any other sport. Golf has many variables that dictate how you play. First, you have different weather and course conditions on a daily basis. How your day has gone before you arrive to the course can have a great effect on how you play. How many times have you been running late all day and then rush to the course to make your tee time only to have quick tempo and a disastrous score? On the other hand, there are days when you arrive at the course early, have a great practice session, and then go out and play wonderfully.

Some things you can control, and some things you can't. Just doing everything correctly doesn't guarantee success, but it sure helps. A former boss once told me that tour players who shoot a course record during a PGA Tour event should find the nearest public course and go play a round before the next tournament round. Essentially, what I am trying to say is, get the bad round out of your system at another golf course rather than in the tournament. This sounds comical, but you rarely see a tour player shoot sixty-two without following it up with a much higher score the next day. The reason this usually happens tends to be the player thinking about how much better he was doing on the previous day versus the present round. Staying in the present and not allowing your mind to wander would be the best way to handle this situation. This sounds easier than I am making it sound, but the more times you are in this situation, the better you will be able to handle your mental game in the future. Even the greatest players in the world struggle, just like the rest of us. Their low scores might be lower than ours, but it is all relative. We all feel the butterflies when the pressure comes.

Many student over the years have asked me why this happens and what they can do about it. I have always responded with this story: One day when I was driving to work, traffic was horrible and I caught every stoplight. When I arrived, my boss was in a bad mood, and so were all the members. The next day, traffic was smooth, my boss was in a great mood, and the members were happy. Now the million dollar question: Did I do anything to cause the traffic to be bad? Could I help it that everyone was in a bad mood? The answer to both of these questions is no. Golf is like life: You never know what to expect or what you are going to get. The only things you can control are your emotions and how you handle these situations.

Here are a few tips to help you the next time you are trying to follow up a great round: Prepare the best you can. Pay attention to the things you can control. Stay in the present and don't let your mind wander. Be happy when you play your great rounds, and don't be so hard on your-self the next day if your game is not as god as it was the day before.

Great Shots and Great Friends Have a Lot in Common

How many great shots do you hit in a round of golf? Most of us if we are honest would say two or three at the most. This doesn't mean that you did not hit good shots; it just means there are very few great shots. Take Tiger Woods at Doral this year, for instance. Tiger hit a three wood from 280 yards to land fifteen feet from the pin to make eagle and go on to beat Phil Mickelson. During Tiger's press conference, he said he hit the shot in the heel. This certainly looked like a great shot in the non-superhuman golfer's opinion, but to Tiger, it was a good shot that turned out better than he thought. When playing a round of golf, whether my score is even par or eighty, there will be only a few shots that were great. That doesn't mean the round did not have good shots; it just means there is a separation between great shots and good shots. The separation in golf is the same in friendships. We all have a number of friends, but we have only a few great friends. The definitions of great friend and good friend are obviously different. Great friends are in your wedding, are there for you during difficult times, and would do anything for you. Good friends are there for you, but you probably wouldn't keep in touch with them regularly if you were to move to a different city.

The message that you should get from this shouldn't be that there are not enough great shots in a round of golf, but just how hard they are to come by. Golf is a game of misses, and where we miss our shots normally determines how we score. Golf is a very difficult game, and we all have different levels of talent. Tiger's 280-yard three wood would be a great shot for me, and one of my shots might be great for a thirty handicap. It is all relative to the player's ability, but the number of great shots is still the same. Remember, cherish your great shots as well as your great friendships, and keep working on both.

Groundhog Day

E very February, the groundhog comes out of his hole and makes the decision how much longer winter is going to be around based on if he sees his shadow. I've watched the movie Groundhog Day with Bill Murray and highly recommend watching it if you like comedy, but I'm not really sure why seeing your shadow would determine weather patterns for the next six weeks. I do know as a golf professional that shadows can be used to help you correct or maintain positions in your golf swing. When the shadows become long early in the morning or late in the afternoon, use some of these examples to check your positions. Your shadow might not be able to weather forecast the weather, but shadows can definitely help your positions in your golf swing.

Target Impact

Rounded Impact

Improper Weight Shift

Perfect Weight Shift

Shadow Putting

Perfect Backswing

Backswing Too Flat

Backswing Too Upright

Hanging with Hank

Last year at the Spirit International's opening ceremony, we asked Hank Haney to be our guest speaker. When I heard Hank was going to speak, I was excited, but when I was asked to pick him up at the airport and take him to the event, I was beyond excited. This was an incredible opportunity for me to pick the brain of one of the best golf instructors on the planet. Knowledge is everything. The more information you can get from people who have been there and done that, the better you will be at your profession. How much better can it get than having Hank Haney in your car for an hour?!

Hank was to arrive around 5:00 p.m. at Hobby AAirport, and I was there waiting for him with a list of questions I had prepared. He came out of the security area wearing jeans and a sweatshirt, hardly noticeable, as I greeted him and introduced myself. We discussed the Spirit and what it means to amateur golf, the Olympic atmosphere of the event, and the golf course—Whispering Pines—where the event was to be played.

Once we arrived at my car and buckled in, I asked him if it would be okay for me to ask him questions about teaching. He told me absolutely, and I pulled out my list of questions. The first thing I told him was "I want to be in your shoes someday as a golf instructor, and I want to find out everything I can in the next hour." I told him there might even be some wrong turns taken to get more information, which he laughed at.

The first question I asked was what it was like the first time he worked with Tiger Woods. He said that Tiger told him before they even started hitting balls "Here are some of the things I disagree with [that] you teach." What do you tell the best player in the world after he tells you that? Hank told me that Tiger now understands those things and obviously has adopted them into his golf swing. Hank is supremely confident in what he teaches, and it takes someone like that to teach the best player in the world.

He gave me many great theories and insight to his world and how someone like him has achieved so much teaching golf. I have been blessed to spend time with many of the top teachers in the game, and they all have incredible insight and knowledge, but Hank impressed me very much. This guy has seen it all and has done it all. When you teach Tiger, have a television series with Charles Barkley and Ray Romano, and still have time to speak at our event and tell an aspiring teacher your ideas, that is pretty cool. There was a moment when I looked over and thought, *Hank Haney is in my car! I am a guy from Tishomingo, Oklahoma, population 4,000, and Tiger Woods's golf coach is in my car!*

I asked so many questions that it would take too many pages to write for this article, but there were a few things I would like to mention. Hank was an incredibly humble person. He asked me after I dropped him off at the hotel if there were any other questions he could answer. He told me we could get together later if I thought of any additional questions. He told me his ideas on becoming a top golf instructor. He told me about his future plans. He told me he was handing the torch to guys like me who were young and ambitious. The question that stands out above all the questions I asked, though, was "What does it take to become the best teacher in the country?" He said, "You already have it." I waited at the edge of my seat, awaiting his answer to what I had. "It's passion!" he said. That one answer will stick with me for the rest of my teaching career. You can have a job or a career, or you can have a passion for something. I haven't accomplished as much as Hank Haney has, but we do have one thing in common. We both have a passion for teaching golf!

How Did I Get So out of Shape?

After a summer of not working out with a metabolism that is starting to change, I noticed my pants were fitting a little tightly around the waist. What happened? I used to be able to eat anything and never worry about weight, but now things are a little different. The funny thing is it did not happen overnight but gradually over time. So my priorities have now changed. I drink more water, eat smaller portions, and exercise. Without a doubt, just a little adjustment in lifestyle and more discipline make a big difference.

This got me thinking about golf swings and the slumps we get into with our games. Our golf games can be compared to almost anything in life. I guess this is why these thoughts continually pop into my head and eventually go on paper. Keeping your body in shape is much like keeping your golf game in shape. If you start to neglect your body, you will see the difference in the mirror. If you neglect your golf game, you will see the difference in your scores. You can coast along for a while neglecting both, but eventually, your metabolism and your golf swing start to slow.

How do you reverse this trend? First, make a commitment to change. Second, find a program that will work with your schedule. Third, stay with the program until you get the results you are looking for. In your golf game and your physical condition, the commitment is the same. Write your goals and desires on paper and put them in a place where you will see them every day. Finding a program doesn't have to be the gym, but having someone to keep you accountable, like a trainer, is always a good thing. In golf, always get a PGA professional to take a look at your swing. Let your instructor know what you want to accomplish, and have him write out a detailed plan to help you achieve this. Staying with your program is the toughest but is a must if you want to keep from fluctuating every month. Consistent weight and consistent scores will let you know if you are sticking to your program.

If you ever visit Whispering Pines, make sure to keep me accountable by asking me what my waist size is and what I shot in my last round.

On second thought, just enjoy the golf course!

Humility, Yips, and the US Open Qualifier

A few months ago, I told my oldest son I was thinking about trying to qualify for the US Open and I wanted him to caddy for me. I'm a golf professional, not a professional golfer, but I love the game and thought why not give it a try! Before I could change my mind, my son had posted on Facebook that I was qualifying for the Open. I'm not a Facebook guy and had no idea the response I would get the next day from teachers at his school, my parents, and everyone else I came in contact with who had read his Facebook page. Most people thought I would be playing in the Open and had no idea what goes into trying to qualify. When people mentioned the US Open, I would tell them I was trying out for *American Idol* the next week! It was actually comical how people reacted to my mythical quest. It felt like *Tin Cup* in many ways and like I was Roy McElroy trying to impress my son rather than the Doctor Lady, as Cheech would say.

As a golf professional, I run the golf operation at Whispering Pines. My job has many responsibilities, just like all golf professionals'. I teach, run tournaments, manage a large staff of caddies and supervisors, play golf with the membership, run a golf shop, and the list goes on. Basically, my job is to make sure that everyone who visits Whispering Pines has a world-class golf experience. Nowhere in my job description does it say I should qualify for the US Open, but how could I pull out now? My son was so proud, and the closer the qualifier came, the more people started finding out. The negative to all of this was that my son couldn't miss school and would not be able to caddy. This was a real bummer because I really wanted this to be a father-son day on the links. The pressure was building, and I thought maybe I should hit some balls and at least practice a little bit.

We hosted the Big 12 Championship a few weeks ago and then had a busy week at the club, so practice was limited, but I did start getting out and playing a bit more than normal. My ball striking was good, and everything seemed to be coming together in my game. This was actually exciting because I play only a few tournaments a year and can usually predict my rounds within a few strokes; they are never going to be really low.

When I first got into the golf business twenty years ago, I played in section events and loved teeing it up any chance I got to play. In college, we qualified or played a tournament almost every week, so tournament golf was just business as usual. As time went gone by and the tournaments became fewer and fewer, anxiety and dread started to creep into my game. If a tournament was on my schedule, the closer it came, the more anxiety I started to feel about posting a score. In the past few years, it has gotten much better, and I have actually played some decent tournament rounds. The crazy thing about all of this is that none of this happens if I'm playing with members or friends or even betting in friendly games on the course. It amazes me what has happened to some of the best players like Ian Baker Finch, David Duval, and even Craig Perks after winning the PLAYERS Championship, but I can relate.

Well, let's get back to the Open qualifier. My first assistant and I traveled to the tournament site and played our practice rounds. It was actually fun, and I felt like I was back in college preparing for a tournament. We played the course as far back as we could play it and hit all types of shots around the green in preparation for the upcoming event. When we finished our practice round, I realized the course fit my eye really well, and I figured that if I had been keeping score, I had shot around seventy-six or seventy-seven. As little as I play, I was actually okay with four or five over par. My main reason for trying to qualify was my son and the fun of what would happen if I got it all going for one round!

Tournament day arrived, and my second assistant was caddying for me because my son had to be in school. I was unusually calm for a tournament round and actually was very focused. The USGA official called my name to the tee, and I started my routine. It wasn't a great tee shot, but we were off and running for a chance at Olympic Club. I hit a very solid hybrid on the long par five for my second shot and ripped a four iron right at the pin coming up just short of the green. I had hit two solid shots and the nerves were in check, but my chip wasn't very good, and two putts later, I made bogey. The next hole was a drivable par four, but I had made up my mind that three wood and then nine iron was my best route to play this dangerous hole. I made a mistake teeing the ball too low and came out of my posture hitting the ball thin and into the water. After teeing up again, I hit a good shot along with a good nine iron but proceeded to three putts. The next hole was another sloppy bogey! Now at the turning point to the round, I smashed a drive on my fourth hole and had 165 yards into the green. My assistant and I agreed that a seven iron was the perfect club. The ball rocketed off the clubface, stopping twenty feet from the pin. At this point, I realized I was not going to have the round of my life, but these two shots gave me confidence that the game was turning around. My caddie and I studied the extremely slick side-hill, downhill, down-grain putt. I breathed on this putt and watched it pick up pace. I watched in disbelief as it rolled ten feet past the cup. The comeback putt for par slid three feet past the cup, and then I missed that putt with a power lip-out that rolled four feet down the hill. Without taking any time, I addressed the putt and missed that one. I tapped the putt into the hole and walked away in total disbelief! I had to ask my caddie what my score was because I honestly did not know.

The rest of the round felt like I was playing in a fog, and then I started yipping numerous short putts on the perfect but extremely fast greens. I fought as hard as I could and played some solid holes on my back nine but just couldn't get anything out of my game. Embarrassment started to set in, and I knew I was about to post one of my highest scores in the past twenty years. Oh yeah, and that Facebook thing, the teachers, my parents and everyone who had some crazy idea that a golf professional who averages seventy-seven on most days was going to qualify for the US Open. John Peterson shot sixty-three that day, and the very best round of my life is still three shots higher than his score.

Me qualifying was never going to happen, but I had never expected to see it happen like it did. When I got home, I was bummed out! My passion is teaching, and I love getting players to reach their potentials. I had students playing in this tournament whom I had coached for this specific event, but I hadn't been able to get my personal game to the level I had hoped for.

When I got home, the family was supportive, and my son was told to stay off Facebook. I put my two young boys to bed that evening as my oldest son and wife went to Target to buy a few things. When they got back, my son handed me a card. The title was "I Believe," and it touched me more than shooting a sixty-three at the qualifier could have. My wife had written on the inside a note of encouragement and about what an inspiration I am to my boys, and my oldest son had written, "It's just an up and down! I've had many! Love, Dylan."

When you put it all into perspective, my score could never compare to the love and support my family gives me. Yes, I shot one heck of a bad round! Yes, I tried as hard as I could on every shot! Yes, I wanted to no card, but what example would that have been to my kids? Who knows, I might try something crazy like this again someday, but this year on Father's Day, I will be at home with my family watching the US Open with the ones I love.

Integrity

We are privileged to have a First Tee program at Whispering Pines. In twenty weeks, we see around 1000 fifth-graders HISDHouston Independent School District. The majority of these kids have never seen a golf course when they arrive. We teach them pitching, chipping, putting, and full swinging over the two nights they are here and try to turn them on to golf. Many of these kids leave with a whole new outlook on the game and with the idea that this sport might be different from all the other sports they have played.

The last evening after all the balls have been hit, retrieved, and put away, they get a speech from me about why golf is the greatest game. The majority of the kids would choose football, basketball, or baseball over golf before the speech, but hopefully, some change their minds when they get back to Houston after two fun nights at the golf course.

First: Golf is a game you can play through your entire life. There are no age limits. We have a ninety-two-year-old man play our course at least once a week. You don't see a lot of ninety-two-year-olds playing football.

Second: Physical size does not necessarily make you better. I usually have the tallest kid and shortest kid stand next to each other and ask the kids who would win in a football game or basketball game. The answer is obvious, but on the golf course, either could compete equally against the other.

Third: Gender does not matter. Annika Sorenstam competed against the guys at Colonial when I was working there. She didn't make the cut but brought more excitement to golf than anyone other than Tiger in the past decade.

Fourth: Golf is a game of integrity. I ask the kids if they know what integrity means. Some say honesty. Some say doing the right thing. I give them a hypothetical example that they all can relate to:

> The coach of the Houston Rockets says to you, "If you make ten free shots in a row, I will put you on the team and give you a

multimillion contract to play for the Houston Rockets." The only catch to this hypothetical example is that the coach would leave the gym and you have to tell him if you made the ten shots. You missed one. It is just one shot. This could change your life, but would you have integrity if you told the coach that you made all ten shots?

You can imagine the look on all of their faces as they wondered what they would do. Then I tell them about PGA Tour Qualifying School and the integrity that some of the players have shown over the years by calling rules infractions on themselves and costing themselves shots at the PGA Tour. The basketball example is not any different from what tour players encounter on the course when their balls move an inch and no one is around to see it. The game of golf is built on integrity. You never see Tiger Woods acting like Terrell Owens. You never see Davis Love acting like John McEnroe, and you never see PGA Tour players in court saying they didn't take a controlled substance and then confess when the heat is turned up.

If our government, professional athletes, and celebrities, along with the rest of us in this great country, had the integrity of professional golfers, the world would be a better place. My desire is to give these children the tools to succeed, and what better way than to give them the game of a lifetime?

Is Your Golf Game Tied up Like a Circus Elephant?

Any of you golfers who have ever been to the circus probably have seen an elephant with a small chain tied around its ankle. It always amazed me that the elephant did not pull the chain out of the ground and just take off. I thought about this and decided to research why this happens. Here is what I found: When an elephant is a baby, the trainers put a metal clasp around its ankle with a chain attached and staked in the ground. When the baby elephant tries to pull away, the sensation is not very pleasant, and the baby is not yet strong enough to pull the stake out of the ground. As the elephant grows, it becomes strong enough to pull the stake out of the ground with no problem, but it does not because it remembers the pain it felt when it was a baby and tried to pull away. The elephant knows just how far it can go before it would pull the chain too tight. It has been conditioned to think it is unable to pull a small stake out of the ground.

It seems crazy that an animal the size of an adult elephant can be held back by something so small.

Is your golf game tied down to the same bad habits you had when you were a kid? Can you never seem to break that scoring barrier? When you see your swing on video, does it look the same as it always did? If you answered yes to any of these questions, your golf game is tied down just like the circus elephant. The bad habits we have when we first start playing golf are usually the same bad habits we have later in life. The chain can be pulled out, and your game can be different! Stop hitting balls on the range for hours if you haven't had a PGA professional tell you what you should be working on in your swing. The more time you spend practicing bad habits, the more you engrain those bad habits.

With a good instructor, you can start to make real changes in your swing. Book a lesson this week with your pro, and break that chain that has been holding you back.

The Jerry Rice Work Ethic

Jerry Rice is considered the greatest receiver in the history of the NFL. The funny thing about Rice is, he wasn't even going to play football in high school. He was persuaded by his coach and turned out to be a star. When Jerry graduated from high school, he wasn't recruited by any of the major programs in the country. He was considered too slow and not strong enough to play for the big programs. Jerry ended up going to Mississippi Valley State, where he set school records. When he went into the NFL draft, numerous teams passed on him, thinking he wasn't NFL material. One team took a chance on Jerry Rice—the San Francisco 49ers. The rest is history!

How did Jerry Rice become, arguably, the greatest receiver in NFL history when all the scouts at every level never believed he was good enough for their teams? Work ethic! Jerry had a legendary work ethic during practice, before practice, and after practice. Jerry performed workouts during the off season that were so grueling that other NFL players tried to incorporate into their own routines but couldn't perform. Jerry's secret was that he worked on his weakest areas as a player. He knew he wasn't the fastest player, so he worked on his routes. He knew he wasn't the tallest receiver, so he worked on his jumping ability to compensate against the other teams larger safety. He also didn't have the largest hands, so he worked out his arms to build strength to be able to hold onto the ball when the defenders would try to strip the ball. He designed a workout specifically for his needs as a player. Jerry Rice knew where he needed to get better and worked tirelessly on the areas, which needed improvement.

In golf, I rarely see players working on their weaknesses. Most people enjoy working on what they do well and neglect the parts of their game that cost them strokes. You need to be well rounded in your practice sessions but also be specific on what your needs are in your game. If you are a good driver of the golf ball, don't stay on the range hitting drivers. I'm not saying to neglect your strengths; rather, minimize the practice time on those areas. If I asked any of you reading this article what the best part of your game and the worst part, you wouldn't hesitate with either answer. If you putt poorly or struggle chipping the ball, then spend more time in those areas. If you are great around the greens but drive the ball poorly, spend more time working on driving the ball more consistently. Pattern your practice around the things that will make you a better player, and you will improve your scores!

Know When to Take Your Medicine

Did your mother ever say, "You have to take all of your medicine if you want to get better"? My mother sure did, and I'm sure yours did also. Now you are probably wondering what taking your medicine and golf have in common. Many times, we make poor decisions on the golf course instead of playing the percentage shot which is in essence taking your medicine. Most big numbers made on the golf course start with a poor tee shot followed by a poor decision. If you hit your tee shot in the woods, you normally have the option to pitch back into the fairway, but most of us try to hit the miracle shot, which usually leads to high scores.

When I worked at Colonial, I spent a lot of time teaching on the range, which runs parallel with the fifth hole, which is considered one of the best holes in America. The tee shot requires a fade off the tee, but most people hit through the fairway and are left with a decision of hitting a miracle shot or pitching back out into the fairway and leaving themselves a one-hundred-yard shot. I would be willing to bet that any golfer given ten shots from 180 yards, having to hit a low hook, with the Trinity River on the right, and a very well bunkered green, would not hit the green more than thirty percent of the time. If you take the same golfer and give him ten shots from one hundred yards, however, I'm willing to bet he would have a much better percentage.

When the PGA Tour would come to town, many of the tour players would be in the same predicament thaat the membership found themselves in every day. The difference was that the tour players would go ahead and swallow their pride and pitch out into the fairway, therefore taking their medicine. When you have a mindset like this, you take the big number out of play. Even when the tour players pitched out the worst scores they made were bogeys. The guys who tried the low-percentage shots normally made doubles and triples. Next time you find your self in one of these predicaments, go ahead and take your medicine and see if your scores don't improve.

Lay-up and Pitch-out Shots

The lay-up shot is one of the most overlooked and least thought-out shots in a round of golf. Most golfers should always lay up unless they have the length to reach the green. Why would you hit a three wood to try to reach a target out of range on a long par five? The other mistake I see quite often is the player, who lays up to one hundred yards. This is a great idea if one hundred yards is your perfect yardage, but many of you reading this try to lay up to this distance and don't have the correct club to get you that far. My fifty-six-degree wedge is a comfortable eighty-five yards, and my fifty-degree is a perfect 110-yard club, so why would I want to lay up to one hundred yards? Figure out your best wedge distance and start laying up to that yardage rather than always trying to la yup to one hundred yards.

The pitch-out shot is the most overlooked shot, in my opinion. The player walks into the trees and uses whatever club is in his hand to hit a shot that either doesn't get him out of trouble or gets him into more trouble. I have done this numerous times and am always baffled that I made such a silly mistake. When you find yourself having to pitch out go through the same process as you would from the middle of the fairway. We often take this shot too lightly and rarely commit to hitting the shot the way it should be played. If you find yourself with a very difficult shot, you usually look at all the options. You process every possibility and then make your decision. When you have a simple pitch-out, you usually don't take the same amount of time to process the shot and end up making silly mistakes like hitting a tree branch you didn't notice, or using the wrong club and hitting it through the fairway into the rough. The pitch-out shot is all about taking your medicine and getting your ball back in play. This shot counts the same as the 300-yard drive and the two-foot putt; they all count as one shot.

The next time you have either of these shots, go through the same process you would on the tee box of a difficult driving hole: Look at all the options, make sure there is a clear path to your target, and commit to the shot. If you do this, your scores will start to drop and the big numbers will disappear from the scorecard!

Look at the Road

Many of us who read instructional articles or watch the Golf Channel usually will go out to the range and try what we have just seen. There is nothing wrong with doing this, but too much information is not a good thing. Research shows that your brain can perform only a few tasks at a time. The more tasks you add, the more complicated something is to perform. I am always amazed by the people who work at fast-food restaurants. They can take an order, get your change, hand you your food, and take another order on their headset at the same time. In golf, this just doesn't work!

Think about when you drive your car to work. We push pedals, pull switches, shift, and rotate things. What would happen if we drove our cars like we play golf? Many of us would crash! You can't think about shifting gears, turning the steering wheel, or pressing a brake. These are things that happen subconsciously. We have done these things so many times, we don't have to think about them. What we need to think about is keeping our focus on the road. If we become distracted or lose focus from the road, we increase our risk of an accident.

So why do we try to think of so many things when we make golf swings? We simply overcomplicate the mechanics of the swing. When you were in driver's education, you had to think about what you were doing in the car with your instructor. Once you received your license, you still would go through your checkpoints before driving, but you didn't worry about where your turn signal was or how to turn on your bright lights. Most of us have graduated from Golf 101 and are ready to get out and drive, but most of us aren't looking at the road. If you haven't graduated from Golf 101, get with a PGA professional and have him help you to perfect the basics. Everyone can have good posture, grip, and alignment!

Once you leave the range, focus on the target only. There are distractions all around you, like trees, bunkers, water, and out-of-bounds stakes. You can choose to focus on all the distractions or keep looking at the target. Once you have committed to your target, the rest of the process is simplified. Leave mechanical thoughts on the range and focus on the road!

Miss the Coin for More Consistent Shots

In the short game, the key factor for consistent chipping and bunker shots is the angle that the club approaches the ball. One of the best ways for me to get my students to impact the ball at the correct angle is to put a coin or something similar directly behind the ball. We used a poker chip for the photos shown of me hitting shots and placed the chip about three inches behind the ball. If the club bottoms out or comes in too shallow, the club will hit the coin every time. This works great for the person who comes in too shallow and blades or chunks shots. The next time you are working on your short game, put a coin behind the ball and watch your short game start to improve!

My One Shot at the Golf Channel

Back in the day, I wanted to be a rock star, just like every teenager on the planet. I was the lead singer in the band Built for Speed, and we were going to conquer the airwaves with our hair-band rock. Well, my quest ended when I had a pretty bad finish in a golf tournament that was followed by a Stryper concert that evening. My dad woke me up the next morning asking what I had shot, already knowing the answer. This is when the big talk happened between my dad and me, and I am not talking about the birds and the bees. He asked me if I wanted to play college golf or be a rock star. The answer was both, but I couldn't accomplish either if I didn't give one of them one hundred percent commitment. It was something I needed to do, but I just didn't want to give up on music. I eventually quit the band and did get a golf scholarship. Now, watching *Behind the Music* and seeing all of those guys from the 1980s all messed up, along with looking at Whispering Pines every day, I realize it turned out to be a great decision.

In my golf career, I have been able to listen to some great stories. One story that has always stood out was a story from Jackie Burke about Jim McClean. Jim was having trouble hitting his driver and asked Jackie for advice. Jackie told him to go down to the ocean and hit some balls into the ocean. Jim McClean took the advice and went down to Galveston and hit some balls into the ocean. He then drove back to Houston and told Jackie that he had hit the balls into the ocean, and he asked what the point was. Jackie asked Jim how he had hit the shots. Jim replied that he had actually hit pretty well! Jackie then said, "It is pretty tough to miss an ocean."

Seve, my all-time favorite, hit pebbles in the ocean with his three iron. This is how Seve learned to be so creative. Once, Seve bet Nicklaus and Crenshaw that he could hit a three iron out of a green-side bunker closer than they could with their sand wedges. They both took the bet and both lost after Seve hit his bunker shot a foot away using a three iron.

He then asked if they would like to bet again. They both declined the offer!

Now why am I rambling away at the keyboard when the title of this article is about the Golf Channel? Well, I decided to send in a video for the Golf Channel instructor search last year. I didn't win the job. Martin Hall was the eventual winner, and he does an incredible job, in my opinion. The stories I've mentioned are all in my YouTube video along with a few other interesting teaching ideas. I thought why not make a fool of myself and play the guitar, hit balls off the beach, and do a few impressions? All of this applied to golf, and the video was a blast to make. Every shot was done in one take except the guitar, because the Golf Channel told me I could not play a Metallica song because of copyright issues, like Metallica was going to watch my YouTube video for the Golf Channel. Anyway, I filmed another guitar part and made sure everything was original. I congratulate Martin Hall for winning, but he still can't play a guitar like me!

If you would like to see the video, go to www.youtube.com and search for Chris Rowe Golf Channel Video 2.

My Trip to the Physical Therapist

G etting old really stinks. Last month, I turned thirty-nine. I will hold at this age for the next fifty years. With age, I have noticed aches and pains that were not there a few years ago. The Advil and Tylenol also get more use than they did in my twenties. A few months ago, I woke up with a pain in my neck that would not go away. I stretched, used heating pads, and tried popping my neck, but nothing really helped. After living with pain for months, I decided to see a physical therapist. I called Dallas Williams in Huntsville and discussed my issues over the phone. He suggested coming in and getting to work on the source of the problem instead of continuing to try the things that were not working.

When I arrived at his office, he identified the problem immediately and went to work on that specific area. We had four sessions together using various techniques to alleviate my pain. After the fourth visit, I felt one hundred percent and have felt great ever since.

Now, how does my physical therapy visit coincide with golf?

My range of motion issues and pain were being caused by one specific problem with my body. When I teach golf, there are always numerous symptoms, but almost always, one specific cause is the reason for the breakdown in the swing. Dr. Williams diagnosed the exact spot where I was having a problem, just like a PGA professional can diagnose a specific swing flaw. When you know exactly what is causing your problem in your golf swing, you can have a specific game plan to improve it. If you are trying to mask it with "Golf Advil" or "Golf Band-Aids," your problem will keep coming back. I could have kept dealing with my pain and lived the rest of my life with a limited range of motion in my neck, or I could do something about it, which I did. Now, every morning, I wake up with no pain. Think about how great it would feel to finally completely eliminate that aches and pains in your golf game.

This year, go to your PGA professional and ask him to identify your main issue in your golf swing. Once he has identified the source of the problem, get your therapy started. Take a series of golf lessons and watch how much you progress. If I had gone to physical therapy only once or twice, I would still have my problem. Keep working on the problem until it has left your golf game for good. It might take two sessions, or it might take six months, but you will never get a better golf game until you diagnose your problem and focus on that area of your game. If your putting is holding you back, dedicate your focus on the putting green. If your swing mechanics have some flaws, get them diagnosed and spend your time working on drills for the specific need in your swing. All of us have some issues in our games; even the guys on the PGA Tour have them. Your golf professional can be your physical therapist for the aches and pains in your game. Give him a call and get your game healthy again!

Pat Green Song

Every once in a while, you hear a song that you play again the moment it ends. My belief about great songs and great golf is that they happen about three times a year. Well, the other day, I was in my office, pricing golf shirts for the shop, and heard a Pat Green song called "What I'm For." This was definitely one of those songs that had a cool sound and a great message. Now, I was in a rock band back in the eighties and could butcher the words to almost any song, so it is not uncommon for me to miss a lyric or two. There was one line, though, in this song that I couldn't figure out for the life of me. I had my teenage son listen three times in a row, and he couldn't figure out what Pat was saying, either. After listening, asking people to listen, and basically giving up, I remembered a website that gave the lyrics to any song. I quickly got on the computer and finally figured out what the second line in the song said. After I read the lyrics, it became clear and made total sense. Now every time I listen to the song, that line is as clear to me as any lyrics you will ever hear. Now, I am not going to tell you what the lyrics to the second line say because all of you reading this would listen to the song and ask why someone wouldn't be able to figure this out, so here is the challenge: Listen to this song and see if you can figure out in the second verse who Pat says he can trust. If you can do this, you have a great ear for music and might not need to read the next paragraph. If you can't figure it out, you probably butcher the same songs I have been butchering since high school.

Now, how many of you go to the range constantly trying to figure out the lyrics in your golf swing? Most of you have done this. You go to the driving range searching for something and usually walk away with the wrong lyrics to your swing and actually think you're singing the correct lyrics. Golfers who do this are the ones who think their swings are on the correct path but really have Band-Aids holding everything together. These people usually play poor rounds of golf and then repeat the process at the range the next day. This approach to practice makes you leave the range frustrated while it engrains even more bad habits. The answer to the lyrics in your swing is your golf instructor. Just like the website that gave me the answer to the songs lyrics, your golf professional has a trained eye to diagnose the problem in your swing. You can have your buddies look at your swing, or you can video yourself and still not come up with an answer. I could have sung this song for the next ten years and had no idea what Pat Green was saying. I chose a website that specializes in lyrics for wannabe rock stars who can't understand the words. Once your golf instructor shows you the correct position or move that you need to make and the balls flies straight, then it all makes sense. Quit trying to figure out the lyrics to your golf swing, and find the golf professional who can help you figure it out.

I bet you can't figure out who Pat can trust!

Pharmacies and the Golf Channel

In a recent lesson, one of my student s asked me if he should straighten his left leg at impact. This was a random question based on what we had been working on in his swing. I answered the question and then asked him why he was thinking this about his swing. He mentioned that he had seen a lesson on the Golf Channel in which the pro had told the student to make this move in the student's swing. I gave my student this example for reading golf magazines and watching the Golf Channel: Both of these outlets for golf instruction are very credible, especially *Houston Links* and *DFW Links,* but everything you read or watch might not be appropriate for your personal golf game.

Every drug in your local pharmacy is good for something, but it doesn't mean all of them are good for you. The fact is, many drugs would really hurt your health if they were not the correct prescription from your doctor. Let's say I walk in to the drugstore and ask for birth-control pills. That would not help me one bit, because I'm a man, but it would be beneficial to a woman who does not want to have children. How about asthma medication for someone who doesn't have asthma? This could speed up the person's heart and make that person feel like he had drunk four Red Bulls. I could use a lot more examples like this, but I would have to call my brother-in-law, who is a pharmacist, to ask him too many questions.

Golfers do this all the time. They watch the Golf Channel and go straight to the range to try the new tip they just witnessed from Hank Haney or read in the article from Jim Flick *in Golf Digest.* If you have been watching *The Haney Project* and decided that because Charles Barkley needs to make his swing flatter, you must make your swing flatter, this will destroy your game if you already swing the club flat. How about the guy who hits the ball with a low trajectory but would love to hit the ball higher? He reads about the stack-and-tilt method and decides this is his new swing, only to find out he can't hit the ball any higher than before.

This article is not about turning off the Golf Channel or canceling your subscriptions to your favorite golf magazines. This article is about you asking your pro what he thinks the new tip you read would do to your golf swing. Just like your doctor knows what prescriptions you should put in your body, your golf pro knows what swing tips you should apply or dismiss in your golf swing.

I read as many articles and watch the Golf Channel as much as any of you reading this article. As an instructor, I am always looking for ways to help your students. These outlets are a great way to gain information but do not always contain the correct prescription for your swing infection. Keep reading, watching, and working on your game; just keep your golf pro in the loop to help you manage through the good and bad prescriptions.

Practice with a Purpose

Many times on the range, I will observe people who are practicing their swings, and the one thing I notice is that people do not practice like they want to play. Take two basketball players—we will call them player A and player B—and watch thier practice habits. Player A works on free shots, making ten in a row, picks the spots where he thinks he will be during the game, and finishes with a few lay-ups. Player B shoots randomly from all over the court. He shoots a few three-pointers and a few under the basket and really has no goals in mind of what he is trying to accomplish. Which player will most likely perform the best in a real basketball game? Player A would obviously play better than player B. On the range, I see a lot of player B. Many of us never pick out a target or have an agenda for what we want to accomplish while on the range. I can't tell you how many times I have been told by golfers, "I hit it great on the range but can't take it to the golf course." The reason I hear this is because a normal driving range is 200 yards in width and the average fairway is forty yards in width. Anyone can hit a drive and have it stay in the range, but fairways are a little tougher. When you practice hitting drives, pick out an imaginary fairway and try to hit the shots in the fairway. When you hit your irons, pick out a green that is the perfect distance for the club you are trying to work on. Try to hit five in a row on the green before you leave the range. When you are about to leave the range, hit a few easy twenty-yard shots to wind down. You never want to leave the range hitting full-throttle drivers. You want to wind down so you don't pull your seven iron on the first hole and swing full throttle, and swing full throttle at a wedge on the second hole. When you gear down before you leave the range, your tempo will be better for the entire round.

When winter arrivesand you go to the range, practice with a purpose. Set goals for the season and write them down. Paper never forgets. Play games to make practice more fun. Try to hit three shots in a row to a green around one hundred yards, then three shots to a green 150 yards away, then three drivers with you imagining that you're on the first tee with all of your friends watching. When you practice with a purpose, you will play like you practice.

Preparation for Tournament Golf

Last year, I started working with the Sam Houston State Professional Golf Management Program. My job is to work with the students in the program who have not passed their playability test. The playability test is required by the PGA for all its members to pass before they can become Class A professionals. The students know the score they have to shoot before they tee it up. In all other tournaments, you are trying to beat the other players, but in this tournament, you are trying to beat a score. It does not matter if you beat everyone you play against; if you don't beat the score, you don't pass. This tournament is a mental test as much as it is a physical test, because the score is always in your mind. Here are some of the ways I prepare these students for this challenge. I hope they can help you with your tournament golf.

The golf swing has to be evaluated and worked on to become as consistent as possible. One thing I am not a believer in is a quick fix. These students are going to get instruction to help their swings for a lifetime. Quick fixes do not hold up under pressure. We look at the swing on video and evaluate the big things in the swing that cause the breakdown. I want my students working on swing changes that will correct their swings, and video is the best way for the student to see this.

The short game is where they all have to work twice as hard as they do on the range. I tell all the students that for every ball they hit on the range, they should hit two putts and two chips. Phil Mickelson spends countless hours on his short game and hits it all over the golf course but still wins tournaments. You can never spend enough time on your short game if you want to play your best golf.

On-course strategy is essential to see how the student performs in a real situation. I take the players to the first tee and ask them to hit three tee shots. They are told they will be playing the worst ball of the three. They continue this process all the way through the hole, hitting three balls for each shot and playing the worst. This shows me how they handle pressure as well as the decisions they make on the golf course.

Remember, almost every big number happens after a poor tee shot followed by a poor decision.

After I have evaluated these three areas, I make suggestions to the students on where they need to spend more time. I give the students specific drills and training methods to help them pass the player ability test.

It is a blast to work with these kids, who have a goal in mind and want to achieve success in the golf business. This is the way I prepare these students for the biggest golf tournament in their careers, and I hope it will help you with your next tournament.

Preparing for a Trip

Recently, my family and I loaded into the car and made a trip to San Antonio. Many of you reading this article have taken family trips, and you probably did a few of the following things: mapped out your trip for the most efficient route, filled the car with gas, checked the oil, had the tire pressure checked, and had an overall inspection of your vehicle before making a long drive. My tires were in need of replacement, so I took my vehicle in for the tires and oil to be changed at a facility where they check all fluids and do a complete inspection. The trip to San Antonio went off without a hitch, and the family had a wonderful time.

Now, how does all of this relate to golf? Preparing to make a golf swing and preparing to make a trip have a lot in common. Your alignment is much like filling your car with gas. Your posture is like having proper tires and air pressure. Your preparation, mental imagery, and routine for your golf shot are much like the map of your trip. If you have a checklist you go through before each trip, the odds of having a successful trip are pretty good. If you have a pre-shot routine, good posture, and alignment, your odds of a good shot have increased. Can you still have a blowout or engine trouble? Sure, you can. Can you go through your checklist in your golf swing and still hit a poor shot? Sure, you can, but the odds have increased in your favor when you prepare.

The average player spends very little time working on the basics before hitting a golf shot. Most players' alignments are way offline and they think nothing of it, but none of us would get in our car and try to drive one hundred miles with a bad tire. If we check out the basics in our setups and routines before each shot, our chances of success will increase, much like they do after we check the basics on our cars before we take trips. Make sure to have regular maintenance on your swing as well as on your vehicle for success on the road and on the links!

Pushing the Envelope

Have you ever been on the golf course and hit your driver perfectly on three consecutive holes? If you answered yes to this question, I would be willing to bet I could predict what happened on the next few drives. More than likely, the fourth swing was a little faster and harder, the fifth shot was even faster and harder, and by the sixth shot, you had swung so hard that you had pushed the envelope on your golf swing. What I mean by pushing the envelope is that you swung out of control to the point where there was no rhythm, tempo, or control in the swing. Why do we do this? The swing was in total control, the ball was flying perfectly, and everything felt great. Why did you try to hit the ball farther? Was 300 yards not far enough? We do these things because the distance we hit the ball is never enough, and we always want more.

Tour players, when playing well, keep the same rhythm in their swings throughout a round of golf. Regardless of the length of the hole or the situation at hand, tour players swing the same. All of the guys on tour have different tempos and swing speeds, but the great ones keep their rhythm the same. Nick Price is a great example of someone who has a quick tempo. Fred Couples is a player who has a beautifully relaxed, smooth swing. If you watch both players practice, you'll see their tempos are the same on every swing. When you watch Tiger play poorly, you see that he changes his tempo and tries to hit the ball too hard. Tiger plays great when his tempo stays the same, however. Regardless of talent, any player can always work on a few things: alignment, posture, and tempo.

Next time you hit a few consecutive good drives, don't try for any extra distance. Accept the distance you are getting, and keep your tempo the same throughout the round.

Watch Fred Funk in any tournament, and you will see why he hits so many fairways.

Putt Like a Twelve-Year-Old

It is interesting to me how complicated adults can make putting. You have teachers who are experts in putting. You have an entourage of teachers around tour players every week making sure their players' strokes are perfect. If you look at the past fifty years of the most dominant players, you'll see that they all had incredible short games. This is, without question, what separates the best players from the players who are trying to keep their tour cards. If you look at Ballesteros, Crenshaw, Nicklaus, Mickelson, and Woods, you see they all had incredible imaginations and consistent routines. These players don't think about a perfect stroke, even though they have all been blessed with great touch and feel.

If you look at the best putters, you see that they have strokes different from each other's. How can Billy Mayfair win tour events with a stroke like his? The answer is that it repeats consistently every time and there is total belief in the method. This led me to a simple discovery this summer when putting against my twelve-year-old son. My son did not think about his stroke, how hard to hit the putt, or how tight his grip was. He simply looked at the hole, made the stroke, and hit the putt near the hole almost every time. In a real game of golf, he could never beat me at his age, but in a putting contest, he could give me a good run for my money. To be honest, I have never given my son a formal golf lesson and will not until he asks for help, but kids see the length of the putt, the slope of the green, and just hit the ball.

Now, if you got in your vehicle to drive and thought about turning the steering wheel, pressing your foot on the gas, and pressing the brakes while driving, you would wreck. You simply look at the road, and the rest takes care of itself. When I teach students about putting, I am really teaching them about getting their minds and eyes working together. Look at the hole when you make a practice stroke. This is the data-collection part of your routine. Your eyes see the target, then send the message back to your brain, and your brain then tells your muscles what to do. If you throw a football or baseball to someone, do you think about what motion your arms and body make? No, you simply make the throw with your arm and your body, and the ball usually goes to or near your intended target.

I am not saying you shouldn't have some basic fundamentals in your putting stroke, however. Your grip pressure should be light, freeing up the tension in your body. Your head should stay steady for two seconds after you have hit the putt. Your thumbs should be on top of the grip, pointing straight down the shaft. Outside of these simple fundamentals, there is not much left to talk about besides your routine.

Here is a game I use with my students that I think could greatly benefit your putting. Use one ball and go around the putting green to every hole. You can't leave a putt short, and you can't three putt. If you do either of these, you have to start completely over from the very first hole. That means if you make it through the first six holes getting every putt to or past the hole and not three-putting and then leave the next putt one inch short, you have to start over at the first hole. This drill will teach you to never leave a putt short and to become very good at the short knee knockers coming back. This game also makes you concentrate on every putt. There have been many times when I have worked on this drill and have come to the fourteenth hole and left it a bit short. Does that mean I hit a bad putt? No, but the putt never had a chance to go in. I have used this drill with hundreds of students, and they all had a difficult time accomplishing the task, but all became better putters.

It is more advantageous to putt with one ball and simulate real golf than it is to putt ten balls with the exact same putt over and over. There are great drills for your stroke, and there are great drills for your game. It is better to work on your game after the basics of your stroke have been fine-tuned. Next time you go to the putting green, forget about mechanics, look at the hole, hit the putt, and pretend you're twelve years old again!

Right Pocket to Left Pocket

Next time you're on the range, try this drill. Set up to a golf ball. Make a backswing going no farther than your pocket. Swing through, with your follow-through finishing no higher than your other pocket. This drill will teach you a number of things about your swing. First, the drill teaches you to rotate. Second, the drill teaches you rhythm and tempo. Third, the drill teaches you to keep your swing short. Fourth, this is a perfect knock-down shot for playing in the wind. When this drill is executed properly, your ball flight should have a right-to-left pattern and your distance should be about eighty percent of a full shot.

On the golf course, try this and you will be surprised where your backswing actually stops. What we feel in the golf swing is normally different than what is really happening. Watch Tiger and Ernie and see where their backswings stop on iron shots. They normally stop at about ear level. When you're on the range, have a friend stand behind you to watch or video your swing and see where your backswing stops using this drill. You might be surprised.

Rock Star Golfer

Most rock stars wish they could be professional athletes, and most professional athletes wish they could be rock stars. I am no Tiger Woods or Eddie Van Halen, but I play guitar almost every evening and obviously have chosen golf as my career. Yes, I did have a mullet in the eighties and was the lead singer and guitarist for Built for Speed. We were going to tour the world with Bon Jovi, but things didn't work out. I am about a four handicap on my music man axis electric guitar, and even though I am a golf professional, my handicap is about a three on the books. These are my two loves when it comes to hobbies.

Most people play golf to relax and to get away from the hectic schedule of life, but some of us lock ourselves in a room and crank up our amps. This drives my wife, kids, and the dog crazy, but for thirty minutes, I am in my happy place.

One evening while jamming away, I hit a chord that reminded me of an old Kiss song. After playing the chord a few more times, I figured out the song. It was like discovering something new that had been right in front of me for years but that I had missed every time because I wasn't listening.

Practice sessions on the range are sometimes like learning a new song. Have you ever heard a player say, "I went to the range and found something"? You hear this all the time from guys who win tournaments and are asked, "What changed in your game?" When golfers go to the range, they seldom have plans or agendas. When you are hitting balls and hit that great shot, do you stop to think about what you did, or do you just rake another ball out of the pile and swing again? Most of my students tend to rake the next ball over and swing. When a student of mine hits that great shot, I always make the students stop and tell me what they felt. Most of the time, they tell me they felt what we were working on in their swing during that particular lesson, but other times, it is something completely different. Teachers can see what is happening in golf swings, but they can't feel what is happening in the swings. *It is very important to stop hitting and to think about why you just hit a good shot.* Going to the practice range shouldn't be a race to see how many balls you can hit. Practice sessions should be a time to improve your swing. If you are not paying attention while hitting balls, you just might miss the key that makes you play great.

The Kiss song was there all the time, and the chord had been played thousands of times, but on that particular day, I was listening instead of practicing. Next time you are on the range, listen to the music in your swing and pay attention to that perfect tone when it happens. Rock on!

Stick Your Pose Like an Olympic Diver

One thing you couldn't pay me to do is to dive from a high platform like the divers in the Olympics! No amount of money could get me up there, let alone get me to jump! I've watched over the years in amazement how the Olympians dive and make it look so graceful. When they hit the water, there is hardly a splash. They are all striving to stick their finish and get tens from the judges.

When you hit a golf shot, you should try to do the same with your finish. I have seen people look like they were dancing after impact. I have seen the fall back on the back foot finish, and I've seen Gary Player walk toward the target finish. Yes, this worked for Gary Player, but it would be better for all of you reading this to try to stick your finish like an Olympic diver. Watch Rory or Tiger after he's hit his shot. He holds his pose usually for a couple of seconds as the ball is still in the air. Sergio takes it to an extreme and holds his pose for an extra amount of time, but this is better than not holding it at all. The next time you play a round of golf, try to stick your finish after every shot, whether the shot is good or bad. Try your best to get tens from the judges as if it were a competition, and I bet you will see better results!

Stop Changing the Radio Station in Your Swing

How many of you, when driving in your car, change the radio station every few minutes? This drives me nuts when my wife does it, but I do it too! Many times after going through all the stations, you come back around and catch the last part of a song you really enjoy. I find this happens with golfers all the time when searching for their swings. A player will take a lesson and work on the changes that the pro asked them to make but then will move on to a different swing thought the next day. You know and I know who you are! Every club has the golfer who will ask the caddie, the starter, and the bag boy for swing advice. I was actually in a pro-am one time and had just finished helping my member on the range when he asked one of our team members to take a look and tell him what he saw. I looked over at the member I had just helped and asked him why in the world he would ask a chemical salesman for swing advice. We all got a big laugh and headed for the first tee! I wouldn't take legal advice from a golf professional, and I wouldn't take swing advice from a lawyer.

One of the quotes I often use when finishing a lesson with this type of golfer is "Don't add anything or take away anything from this lesson." The next time you take a golf lesson, listen to the entire song instead of changing the station. You never know if your favorite song is about to be played or if your best round ever is about to happen, so don't change that station!

Surgery, a Canceled Flight, and a Spider Bite

Have you ever had one of those months when things just were not going your way? We all have, but this last month for me has been historic. Each summer, I take a group of our members to Northern Michigan to play a home-and-away match. Great weather, a good golf course, and fellowship always make for a good trip. After our tournament was over, I went to Traverse City Airport to fly back to Dallas. My family and I had gone to Fort Worth to visit before my trip, so I had decided to fly out of DFW instead of Houston. Once I arrived at the airport and saw lots of people standing around, I knew my flight was most likely delayed or possibly canceled. After two hours of standing at a counter and trying to get on a different flight, I submitted to the reality that I was stuck in Michigan until the next morning.

The next morning, I arrived at the same counter where I had stood for two hours the previous day. It was amazing that the lady actually remembered me and called me by name. (Just joking on the amazing part!) Now she told me that I might not get out of Michigan until the next day. With many clicks on her computer, she found a flight to Dallas connecting out of Chicago. Thank you, Lord! Off to the gate I went, and I arrived in Chicago.

Once I got off the plane in Chicago, I started looking around for the gate of my connecting flight. To my bewilderment, there was no such flight. I then pull out my ticket to look at the itinerary and realized the lady had given me incorrect information and I was flying to Houston, not Dallas, in twenty minutes. I raced to the gate and got there just in the nick of time. I reached for my cell phone to call my wife and let her know what was going on, and true to Murphy's law, my cell phone would not work.

The plane took off and flew over my home in Huntsville, and then I boarded another plane in Houston to fly back over my house again to get to Dallas. Once arriving in Dallas, I retrieved my car and headed south to see the family. Twenty-seven hours later, I arrived!

The next day was great until my stomach started hurting extremely badly. Four hours went by without the pain stopping, and I went to the emergency room. Six hours later, I was in surgery, getting my appendix removed. How was this week going?

Two weeks later, I woke up in the middle of the night with my finger itching. The next day, my finger started turning black and I realized I had been bitten by a brown recluse. After three rounds of antibiotics, the finger still works.

Now to the golf part of this story! How many times have you started off a round of golf making a couple of birdies? This was the beginning of my trip to Michigan. How many times do you make a few bogies after the birdies, but have a round that is still okay? This was my flight being canceled, but one of my members let me stay with him at his lake house in Michigan. How many times toward the end of the front nine to do you make a few big numbers on the scorecard but know you can turn it around on the back nine? This was finally getting home and seeing the family. The back nine was all snowmen! This was surgery and a spider bite. Now, some of you reading this have had a few rounds on the course like my real-life story.

You can choose to tee it up again and know it could never be that bad, or you can choose to never fly on a plane, to check the bed for spiders every night, and to carry three cell phones just in case one quits working.

The moral to this story is that you can't live your real life or let your score dictate getting back out there and giving it another shot. Your life and your golf game might be in shambles, but you might be one birdie away from changing it all. Life and golf can beat you down at times, but you have to stay positive and look at the glass as being half full, not half empty. The only thing in life that we can control is our attitude. I will bet that my travel experience will never be that bad again, and now every time my flight is on time, I will appreciate it more. When I have a horrible round of golf, I will appreciate the birdies more the next round. Keep it all in perspective and laugh about it on those tough days. The only thing I could control this month was how I reacted to my circumstances. Now, looking back on the whole debacle, I appreciate my health more, I'm still terrified of spiders, and the next golf trip is already booked!

Take the Left Side out of Play

Have you ever watched a PGA Tour event and seen a player hit a shot that looked like it went five miles right but landed by the hole? The camera always makes the player look like he just hit the farthest right shot of his life. This is an illusion, and the proof is where the ball actually lands. If you have ever gone to a PGA Tour event, you have noticed that the majority of the players miss their shots to the right of the target. You will seldom see a tour player pull a shot to the left. This is because of the player's angle of approach to the ball. Jim Furyk's swing is all over the place, but the downswing is very shallow and comes from the inside. This is what allows him to hit the ball as well as any other player on tour. If your downswing path is from the inside, you can hit the ball too far right, but your path will never allow the left side into play unless you flip your hands; however, if you don't rotate your body, meaning the right shoulder, right pocket, and hand, you will be in the woods instead of the fairway.

When I am giving a lesson, I want my student to completely take the left side out of play. The best thing my student can tell me after his first lesson is that he did not miss anything to the left. Well, what if there is a lake to the right of the green? Okay, use common sense and play the smart shot, but under normal circumstances, try to hit your shot between your target and five yards right of your target. A blocked shot will play better than a pulled shot any day of the week and twice on Sunday. If you can eliminate one side of the golf course, your chances to score improve tremendously. I am not saying to hit every shot way right of your target, but I am saying your miss should be to the right, not to the left. You can swing as far right as you want as long as you rotate your body back to the target. If you stop rotating, you will hit the ball too far right.

The next time you are on the range, imagine playing a shot into the eighteenth green at Pebble Beach. The waves from the Pacific are rolling into the sea wall, and you have only one ball left. If you had this situation, you would do your best not to pull your shot in the ocean. Hit the ball and see if you would have landed on the green or made a splash. Do this several times until all your shots have landed in an area either five yards right of your target or right at the target. When you can do this without hitting left, you have taken the left side of the course out of play and have given yourself the best opportunity to score.

Target Impact and Rounded Impact

Target impact is considered by many as a two-plane or upright golf swing in today's modern terminology. Many swings pre-Pro V1 golf balls were considered target impact. To hit the ball long with persimmon woods and soft balata balls, the players had to swing out to right field and create speed with the hands. I even had an article published in *Golf Digest* telling people to swing to right field back in the mid nineties, with the help of a great guy named Hunki Yun. This is one of the reasons that guys like Seve Ballesteros and Greg Norman were hitting 300-yard drives in the 1986 Masters. Target impact is determined by where the club points right after impact and relies on timing and hand rotation. In the target-impact position, it doesn't matter if the backswing was upright, flat, or perfectly on the shoulder plane, but only where the club direction is going after impact. Jack Nicklaus, Tom Watson, Seve Ballesteros, Greg Norman, Hale Irwin, and Phil Mickelson all have this after-impact position.

Rounded impact would be considered today's modern golf swing. Rounded impact by definition is when the club starts to work immediately left of the target after impact. This impact requires very little hands or timing but relies on body rotation to square the face. The tour players today rotate their upper and lower bodies extremely fast to generate club head speed while swinging as hard left as they want without fear of hitting the ball left. This is completely opposite of what most golf instructors taught up until equipment changed and the great courses of the world became too short. Today's golf balls do not spin nearly as much, and bulge and roll on a driver is a term that most college golfers have never heard of. In a rounded impact swing, the backswing is usually flatter or on the shoulder line, but that is not always the case. Fred Couple and John Daly both have rounded impacts with extremely upright backswings. Once again, backswing does not determine which impact you fall into in all cases!

Tiger Woods is the only player I have seen who actually uses both of these impact positions. Tiger has a rounded impact position with his irons and has target impact with his driver. This, in my opinion, is why he struggles so much with his driver. The swing speed he produces can't be timed out with hands. Have you ever seen him hit a bad stinger two iron? He always hits this shot great because he matches his lower and upper body through impact and then goes immediately left. With the driver, he has a two-way miss because he is timing his impact.

Physical ability and flexibility have a tremendous effect on which impact category a player will fall into. Many of the players mentioned in target impact have had back or hip issues. This impact puts a lot of strain on these two areas. Most players fall into their impact positions based on how much rotation their hips can physically make after impact. This is usually based mostly on genetics and their physical makeups. Sometimes through physical therapy or working out, a player can increase his movement in these areas, but most of the time, the player should use the principles for which impact he falls into.

Here are some of the main principles to be aware of after determining which impact position you are.

Target impact
Weight transfer should be to the right side on the backswing for the right-handed player.
The player should make a full shoulder turn with back facing the target to allow for timing needed at impact.
Transition from the top of the backswing to the start of the downswing needs to be smooth and cannot be rushed.
Swing more to right field with less hip rotation.
Rotate your hands and forearms just before impact.

Rounded Impact
Weight transfer does not have to be completely on the right side for a backswing.
Your downswing should be aggressive, with the hips and shoulders turning to shortstop position at the same time rather than right field like in the target impact.
Rounded-impact players need to stay in their postures as long as possible.
Use very little hands at impact.
Swing as hard left as you want, and the ball will go straight if you continue turning and stay in your posture.

Target Impact

Rounded Impact

The Fifty-Percent Golf Swing

Every once in a while, you receive a tip that changes the way you swing the club. I was recently on the range with one of my assistants, and he gave me a swing thought that made too much sense. I took out his driver and started hitting a few shots without any warm-up. The first three shots were perfect, down the middle, a little draw, and 290 yards. The fourth swing was a different swing altogether. Because the first three shots were exactly how I had envisioned them, I felt the need to try to swing harder on the fourth. After three more wayward shots, my assistant told me I was swinging too hard and too fast. He then told me to swing fifty percent. To my surprise, every fifty-percent shot was going down the middle and landing within ten yards of my one hundred-percent swings. This isn't a brainstorm, and all of us teachers have used drills like this to help our students, but here is where I decided to take this drill to the next level.

A few days later, I went down to River Oaks to look at its incredible teaching facility and get ideas for the one we were going to build at Whispering Pines Golf Club. I was playing with one of my assistants and Robert Thompson, who is on the Senior PGA Tour. Before we arrived at the golf course, I had told both of them I was going to swing only fifty percent the entire day. This sounds like it would be easy, but when you are playing with two very talented players who hit it a long way, it is difficult to stick to your game plan. On the first hole, they both hit great drives and I proceeded with my fifty-percent swing, leaving my golf ball about ten yards behind. This process continued the entire day, and my shots actually started to reach their tee shots, and the distance I thought was lost came back with less effort. For the entire round, I tried not to watch any of their shots because of the alpha-male ego that would surely make me swing harder than necessary. When the round was over, I evaluated my performance. The entire goal for the day had been to play eighteen holes swinging at fifty percent. When it was all said and done, I played fourteen holes at fifty percent and the other four holes at more than fifty percent. On some of the holes where I wasn't able to stick to my game plan, I made bogeys and some pars. The score did not matter as much as the game plan set forth on the first tee.

Here is my belief and the reason for this article: A perfect golf swing that is rushed has very little chance to repeat with consistent solid contact. A golf swing with a few flaws but with good rhythm has a much better chance of repeating. It seems like every week, I see Tiger Woods swinging as hard as he can with his driver and immediately yelling fore right! I don't think Tiger will ever call me for a lesson, but if he ever did call for a lesson, I would give him the same tip my assistant gave me: Slow it down, swing fifty percent, and watch how consistency comes back to your game.

A Slow Transition Can Make All the Difference in Your Downswing

As teachers, we sometimes make the mistake of teaching students what we are working on in our own games. Every once in a while, I have a brainstorm that seems to make such a difference in my own game that I have to share it with my students. So this is my latest epiphany: a slow transition of the downswing. It does not matter how technically perfect you are at the top of your backswing if you can't make a smooth transition into the downswing. Here is a thought for the next time you are on the range: When you reach the top of your backswing, have a one-second pause and then begin the downswing. If you are like me, one second feels like an eternity to you, but in reality, you probably are not even stopping for one second. Remember, what you feel and what's real are usually different. By pausing for a second, you really have to rotate your body through the shot if you want to hit the ball solidly. Try this and see if it doesn't help your game.

The Big Fish Theory

Since coming to Whispering Pines, I have taken up fishing, mainly because one of our members always has two fishing poles and wants me to throw a few while his wife hits her golf shots on the fifth hole. Fishing has never been a passion of mine, because of my lack of patience and skill, but it has been enjoyable at times when the fish are biting. One thing I've noticed while fishing is that rarely does a fisherman catch a big fish and then leave the fishing hole. They invariable throw a few more thinking they will catch a bigger fish.

This happens on the driving range as well. If I had a dollar for every time a golfer hit a great drive on the range and then teed up ball after ball trying to hit the big one again, I would have a few extra dollars in my bank account. When players hit the great drives during their practice sessions, they should put the drivers away and hit a few wedges or putts before they go to the first tee. Unfortunately, most people keep swinging, trying to catch that monster fish of a drive, and never do repeat that shot. The outcome is people swinging harder and faster. Before long their entire rhythm and timing is gone. These golfers go to the golf course swinging out of their shoes and never find the rhythm they had when they were first warming up on the range.

The next time you go fishing and catch the big one, admire the fish, take a picture, put it back in the water, and move on! The next time you are warming up before your round and hit the perfect drive, admire the shot, take a mental picture of what you just did, and move on to the putting green!

The Blowout

A few months ago, I went to the store where I purchase my tires and asked to have them rotated. The drive from Huntsville to Whispering Pines puts a lot of miles on my vehicle, so I stop by and have the tires rotated every three months. The gentlemen who rotated the tires came out to tell me it was about time for a new set and that the tires didn't have too much life left in them. I asked, "How much longer do you think I can make it, because I don't have a lot of time right now to wait on replacing them." He told me I could probably make it until the next rotation, but not any longer. I shook his hand and told him I would be back in a few months.

About two weeks later, my wife and I decided we were going to go on a date and headed toward the Woodlands. As we were driving, I felt my car start to pull to the left and realized I had probably had a blowout. In all my years driving, I'd never had a blowout and really wasn't sure what to do. I knew there was a spare tire in my trunk with a lot of tools that I didn't know how to use. We immediately pulled the car off the highway near a rest stop. The Lord was really watching over me, because no more than a half mile down the highway, major construction had started on I-45 and there would have been no place to pull over. I looked, fumbled, and finally found all the tools along with the spare tire and began the process of changing my first flat. After thirty minutes in the dark, getting filthy, and exhausting myself, I had changed my first flat. My wife looked at me and asked, "What are we going to do now?" I said we were going on a date! We reached the restaurant and immediately both made our way to the bathroom to wash up. We had a great meal and felt very blessed and fortunate that nothing bad had happened.

I'm always finding stories in my life that parallel golf. Many golfers are told they should get their swings looked at before they have blowouts. Most golfers wait until they are headed down the I-45 fairway before they realize something is wrong with their swing. The technician at the tire store is like your golf professional. My technician told me I was going to have an issue, and I chose to wait and chance something happening. I know many golfers who think they can wait and put off getting their golf swings' tires changed. Having an accident in your car obviously is much worse than having a bad round of golf, but you can learn a lot from what happened with my blowout. Get regular maintenance on your golf swing, and don't wait for a major issue to happen. You don't have to get new tires every year, and you don't have to take a lesson every day, but it is in your best interest to get your regular maintenance on both. The next time you feel your swing pulling off that I-45 fairway, call your golf professional and make an appointment to get your swing back in the center lane.

The Golf Thermostat

The job of a thermostat is to regulate to a desired temperature. In our house, we keep the thermostat set on seventy-three in the summer and seventy in the winter months. Most people probably do the same within a degree or two. We all have temperatures we are comfortable with. When playing golf, we all have scores we are comfortable with as well. How many times have you gone out and shot much higher than normal on the front nine and then played much better on the back nine to shoot a score very close to your average round? The same happens in the opposite fashion, when you play incredibly on the front nine and then go shoot a higher than normal second nine to average out very close to your eighteen-hole average.

We all have thermostats built into our golf games. Each of us is comfortable with a score, and each of us tends to work our way back to the comfort-zone score, whether it be up or down. When we set our thermostat in the house at seventy-three and the temperature rises above the setting, the air-conditioner will kick on to bring the temperature back down. So what is your golf thermostat set on? We all have our numbers! My number is usually seventy-six, and the majority of the time when I play, I will score within a few shots of my comfortable setting. PGA Touring professionals have much lower numbers, but they still have their golf thermostats. How many guys have you seen on television shoot incredible front nines and the announcers start talking about fifty-nine? Usually, the player shoots a much higher score on the back nine and averages out within a few shots of his normal good round.

If we all have golf thermostats and we can set them to whatever temperatures we decide, why don't we all set them lower? One of my students won an event after getting off to his usual bad start. He digs himself a hole and then works his way out. His golf thermostat is set between sixty-eight and seventy-two, and this is the number he usually scores. He asked me how to fix this, and I told him to lower his thermostat and change his comfort level.

Whether you shoot in the nineties or the sixties, you can change your thermostat. Think about what your real golf thermostat setting is on. Be honest about your number and then decide to lower the temperature by five degrees. Change your thermostat, and your scores will start dropping like a cold front in January!

Dream big and work harder.

The Golfer Who Lost His Game

Each year, we have a home-and-home match with the Wade Hampton Club in North Carolina. We fly out to the mountains in North Carolina in the summer, and their team comes to Whispering Pines in November.

The matches always place the two golf professionals playing each other the final day. Pete Matthews is the Wade Hamptom Club's professional. He's a very accomplished player. He's made the cut in a PGA Tour event along with a long list of impressive accomplishments. One of Pete's great traits as a player is that he is humble and doesn't talk about his game. But make no mistake, he is a competitor and wants to win.

During our match, I was really struggling with my game and getting absolutely waxed. As a teacher, I'm always interested in getting more knowledge for my students and have no problem asking the guy beating my brains out about some of his ideas.

One intriguing question prompted this article. On the eighteenth hole, I asked, "Have you ever been in a slump, and if so, how did you get out of it?"

Pete told me he had won numerous tournaments in college and in one event had totally demolished the field and won by a record margin. On the very next event, he had shot 88–89–89. He was one of the best college players in the country and had just shot the highest scores of his college career.

Now I was very interested, because this game I was witnessing wasn't anywhere close to those scores. In response to my question, he told me in his southern drawl that he had gone to the golf course every morning and teed it up. He had played one ball and played for a score every time. This was not an immediate fix for his problem, but it was a start. He had played every day until he was able to break 80. Now remember, this guy was one of the elite college players in the country. Eventually, the scores started to drop even more, and a few months later, he was shooting the scores that resembled those of the player he had been.

There is no question his game was back, and it amazed me how candid and open he was about a horrible time in his golf career. Pete got his game back and then some, but he could have hung it up and never played again. The greatness about this story is that the golfer did get out of his slump and went on to become an even better player.

We all go through slumps in golf if we play this game long enough. Tiger and Jack have lost more times than they have won. The history of this game will show you how difficult it is to play at a high level all the time. Pete's story should be an inspiration to all of you going through slumps. Keep a good attitude, work on your game, and push through to the other side!

The Perfect Pot of Stew

One of the things I love to do is cook, and one of my specialties is vegetable beef stew. When the weather starts to turn cold, there is nothing better than a hot bowl of stew and sweet cornbread. I make it with fresh carrots, potatoes, corn, peas, onions, stewed tomatoes, and brown hamburger meat with all my special seasonings. I'm getting hungry writing this article!

A few weeks ago, the weather turned chilly and I headed for the store for the ingredients to make a batch of stew for the family. As I started making my savory specialty, I started experimenting with a few new seasonings. I'm still not sure why I varied from the normal, but I did. I then reached for the salt and began to pour it into the pot without measuring. My biggest blunder was about to happen! I never took a taste test to see how the finished product might turn out. I poured the piping-hot stew into the bowls and put them on the table for the family. This kind of sounds like Goldilocks and the three bears, doesn't it? As my wife and kids took their first bites, I knew within seconds my bite would not taste good. Everyone almost simultaneously said yuck. I then took my first bite and understood what had happened. I had tried to become creative with something that was already good and had not testing the finished product before putting it out. If I had worked in a restaurant, I would have been fired! I did everything to try and make it better, but eventually, we all ate something else and my yellow lab had a lot of salty stew.

How does this relate to golf swings? How many tour players win tournaments or have the best years of their career and change swing instructors or switch club companies? Why can't we leave well enough alone? It is much like my perfect pot of stew; I didn't need to do anything different. You stick to the recipe that works. I knew a tour player who had his most successful year and then switched club companies the next season and completely lost his game. Yes, his contract was great, but he couldn't play with the new clubs, and he hasn't been the same since. Look at Padrig Harrington! He won three majors and decided to change everything about his game. Byron Nelson said, "Find the swing that works for you and spend the rest of your life trying to perfect it."

If you have been swinging well for a long time, there is no need to make a drastic change. Can we all use a little more or a little less salt every once in a while? Sure, we can! The object of this game is to always try to improve, but a major overhaul isn't always necessary. Golfers should always have maintenance on their swings. The minimum you should see your instructor should be once a month in the off season and at least twice a month during tournament season. If your swing has never been great and you never achieved much success in golf, then have your instructor show you how to make stew! If you like the way your stew tastes, keep making it!

This winter when you eat that perfect bowl of stew, think about your golf game for 2013 and make it your best year ever!

The Pool Table

My wife and I recently celebrated our ninth wedding anniversary. With three kids and busy schedules, it is tough to find time to hang out as much as we would like, but we were going to have a nice anniversary no matter what. I called my wonderful mother-in-law and asked if she would keep the kids so I could take her daughter out on the town. She, being the great grandmother she is, said no problem. I booked a hotel room at our favorite hotel in Dallas, and off we went.

We had a wonderful twenty-four hours without kids and really enjoyed the time we spent together. We went to Snuffers and had the best cheese fries on the planet, then had dinner at Bluefish sushi bar. After dinner we went back to the hotel and went to the game room area, where there was shuffleboard and a pool table. My wife wanted to play pool, so we both grabbed a couple of cue sticks and started a game. It did not take long to figure out that my wife's handicap at pool was around twenty-five. Now, I am not saying I am a pool shark by any means, but I have played enough to consider myself decent.

After a few games, she asked me to show her how to play. I highly discourage husbands from teaching their wives how to play any sport. We could start talking about our rounds on the golf course together, but I will leave that for another article. I have personally never tried to explain how to play pool to anyone, but as I'm a golf professional, I figured she could only get better with instruction. We talked about the basic way to hold the cue stick and then talked strategy. Now here is where the golf part comes in.

In a game of pool, the idea is to hit all of your balls into the pockets, with the eight ball being the last one to fall, before your opponent can accomplish the same goal. Much of the strategy involved in pool is setting up your next shot. If you make a shot but have nothing for your next shot, you did not think out your strategy very well.

In golf, we should use the same type of strategy when playing a round. Every pre-shot routine should go through this thought process:

What is the wind doing? What type of shot am I trying to play? Where do I want to be for my next shot? This routine is the way PGA Tour players play each shot.

Many holes at Whispering Pines require being on the correct side of the fairway for the best approach into the green. Our tenth hole is a great example of this. The tenth green is long and has a large hump in the middle. If the pin is placed on the back right corner, a shot from the right center of the fairway has to carry a couple of towering pine trees to reach the green. If the tee shot is placed on the left side of the fairway, the second shot is pretty much a straight shot. When standing on the tee, you should always look towards the green to decide what type of shot you will try to play. Many times, it is better to miss on the correct side of the fairway than to hit your best drive on the wrong side of the fairway.

Ben Hogan was probably the most strategic player to ever play the game. He would dissect every inch of the golf course during his practice rounds and would never vary from his strategy. In the book *The Match*, Hogan laid back on the par five tenth hole at Cypress Point when he had an opportunity to go for the green in two. His strategy was to hit a wedge from his perfect wedge distance rather than to go for the green in two and possibly face a tough bunker shot if the shot was not hit perfectly. If you have read the book, you know he holed the shot for eagle, which ultimately was the difference in the match.

The next time you are on the golf course, think about where you are trying to place the ball in the fairway to give yourself the best opportunity for your approach.

By the way, if you are wondering how the game of pool ended up with my wife... I scratched on the eight ball!

The Pot Roast

First, I want to begin this article by telling everyone how much I love my mother and how wonderful a cook she is. Second, my mother will never be allowed to read this article.

All my life while I was growing up, my mother would have dinner on the table at 6:00 every evening. I have made this same dinner ritual at my own home. It is important, in my opinion, to have dinner as a family, not just on holidays or special occasions, but on every evening possible. My mother would spend her Sunday mornings before church preparing a roast. She cooked the roast in a crock pot with potatoes, carrots, onions, and seasoning. I thought my mom made the best pot roast on the planet. Now here is where my mother needs to turn the page of her *Houston Links* magazine. My mother-in-law, Pam, makes her roast differently and, I have to say, much better! Pam sears her roast to seal in the juices, puts it in the oven for hours, and then adds the potatoes and carrots toward the end of the cooking process. My first time eating this meal was fantastic! I never realized what I had been missing. The meat melted in my mouth, and the juices exploded my taste buds. This, by far, was the best roast I had ever eaten. My wife makes her roast the same way for the family, and it tastes just like her mom's.

If I would have never eaten my mother-in-law's roast, I would have just assumed my mother's way was the only way to cook a roast. What you learn or are taught at a young age usually stays with you. This is a wonderful thing, unless you were taught how to do something incorrectly or not as well as possible. In this case, the way my mother cooked was not a problem at all, but after trying something different, I realized there was a better way.

In our golf swings, we sometimes stick to old-school philosophies rather than trying something new. If trying something new doesn't work, you don't have to keep trying to make it happen, but when it does work, you might just have found your new secret recipe for your swing. I don't believe in the perfect golf swing, but I do believe that everyone has his own perfect swing. The key is to find your own perfect swing. If you never try something different and just stick to the same old-same old, you will never know how much better you could get.

My mother's roast was under par on any course, and that would make most people happy every round, but my mother-in-law's roast was a course record. Explore different possibilities with your swing the next time you are on the range. I personally never try to give the same lesson twice and always try to come up with better ways for my students to play.

The next time you have a pot roast, think about your golf swing becoming better, but don't ever let your mom know that your mother-in-law's is better!

The Speech

My son Pierce goes to Alpha Omega Academy in Huntsville and is in the second grade. It amazes me what the kids are learning at such a young age. Pierce came home a few months ago with a speech he had to memorize. The speech was "Going to Bed," and the length of the speech was extensive. I couldn't imagine trying to memorize anything that long with my forty-year-old brain. All the students would have to memorize their individual speeches and speak in front of their class-mates, judges, and parents. For many people, public speaking is the great-est fear.

The first step to my son learning his speech was memorizing the first half until he could say it perfectly. After a week of going over this every night, he had it down. The second step was to learn the last half of the speech. We spent a week learning this and soon had it down perfectly. Then it was time to combine both halves to see if he could say the entire speech without making any mistakes. This entire process took about one month of constant work. After we had the speech down, we simulated what it was going to be like when he actually had to get up and speak in front of the judges. My wife and I called his name just like they would in the speech meet. We had him stand in front of us and go through his entire speech with the family watching. When he finished the speech, we clapped and cheered just like they would do in the speech meet. We tried to make his practice as real as possible so he would know what to expect when he was actually in that situation.

In our golf games, we should pattern our practices and work on our games like my son did for his speech. The first part of your golf progress should be by learning the game in stages, the basic fundamentals of the golf swing and working with a PGA professional to achieve the correct swing path. The second part of your golf progress should be in the short-game area. You should be able to hit all shots around the green and from the sand along with putting. Once you have put all of this together, you are ready to practice like you want to play on the course.

When you practice, you should simulate what you might encounter on the golf course. You should hit every shot with a purpose. You should put yourself in situations like having to make five putts in a row on the putting green so you know you can make the putt on the course when it matters. You should hit three drives in a row just like you would want to hit off the first tee before starting your round. You should hole a chip shot on the chipping every time you practice so you know you could do it if you had to hole a shot on the last hole to win a bet.

All of these suggestions are to prepare you just like we were preparing Pierce for what he was going to encounter in his speech meet. The better you prepare, the better your ability to perform. If you take each piece of your game and try to perfect it, piece it all together, and then practice like you want to perform, you can have success!

By the way, Pierce finished in the top three and went on to the regional speech meet!

The Spirit of the Game

Every two years, we host the Spirit International Amateur at Whispering Pines Golf Club. Most people don't know too much about this tournament, and neither did I when I lived in Fort Worth. I have been very fortunate and blessed to work at great courses and to be around wonderful tournaments, but this one is different from all the others.

What makes the Spirit different from tour events and club tournaments are the accommodations where the players stay and the attitude of the players. If you play on the PGA Tour, you stay at the nicest resorts and best hotels in the world and have a Cadillac to drive for the week. To say you can become spoiled playing the tour is an understatement. However, the ninety-six kids who play in the Spirit all stay at Camp Olympia, which is part of our property at Whispering Pines.

Camp Olympia is incredible, but the sleeping arrangements are not the Four Seasons. The teams bunk with other teams from around the world. Can you imagine walking into your hotel room and seeing two guys from Sweden and two guys from Australia rooming with you? This is what happens to these kids when they arrive at camp. By the end of the week, these kids have formed friendships that probably would never have happened on the golf course. The kids also go to some of the Houston First Tee programs and help beginning golfers with their golf swings along with sending medical supplies back to their home countries to the less fortunate.

Corby Robertson had a dream to have an Olympics of golf. He built an incredible golf course and had his tournament come to fruition. These kids leave Whispering Pines with an understanding about relationships and the spirit that is within all of us. The golf tournament is wonderful to watch, the participants are the stars of tomorrow on the PGA and LPGA Tours, and the friendships they form last a lifetime. The big-tour players could learn a lot about life and friendship if they played more tournaments like the Spirit International Amateur.

The Storm

A few months ago, I was playing golf with a buddy of mine just north of Fort Worth. On the way home, I could see a massive thunderstorm directly in my path. There was really no way for me to get around the storm . The raindrops started to pitter patter on my car, and before long they had turned into a downpour. Cars were pulling over, the wind was howling, and my windshield wipers were going full speed. The rain was coming down so hard that my car was going at a snail's pace to ensure my safety. This intense rain lasted about five minutes and then was gone. The skyline of Fort Worth was beautiful with the sun gleaming off the skyscrapers with ominous dark clouds now in my rearview mirror.

Golf can sometimes be like the storm I went through. You can be cruising along with the sun shining when a few rain drops start to creep into your game. Before you know it, you are in a downpour with your game and just can't see any way out. We have all been there! I have wanted to quit this game more times than I can count. Then you see a ray of sunlight. We all go through storms in our golf games and in real life. If you do all the necessary things, like turning on your headlights and windshield wipers and slowing your speed, you will usually come out of these storms just fine. The same is true in golf; go see your golf professional for a lesson, put in some extra practice time, be patient, and wait for your storm to pass.

Think of Steve Stricker and what he has gone through with his game. He definitely went through some storms, but he came out of them and has played some incredible golf in the past few years. Tiger has gone through some self-inflicted storms, and Phil has had some difficult storms come his way that he had no control over. Both of these guys will more than likely be on top again. My personal game was at an all-time low a few months ago, but with some hard work, change of attitude, and some tweaking of the swing, I am playing some of the best golf I have played in years.

We will all have storms pop up in our golf games. Nobody plays great all the time. It is just a game, so keep that in perspective. The next time you feel like you're going through a storm in your golf game, turn on your lights, get those windshield wipers going, and drive through it!

Bad Swing and Great Mind

Years ago, I met a guy who came to me for a golf lesson. In all of my years teaching, I don't think I'd ever run across a guy like this one before. His swing was all over the place. He had too many flaws to even start to describe, but he did have the most positive attitude I have ever seen. Any time we would go to the range to work on his swing, he would hit some pretty ugly shots but could always find something good about the ugly shots. He would hit a big fade and miss the practice green by a mile but tell me how good his trajectory was. He would yank the ball left and have it fade back to the green and tell me that was exactly what he was trying to do.

As a teacher, this could have been the most difficult lesson I had ever faced, or it could have been the best. I took the same positive attitude and fed his ego on how great he hit the ball. Of course, I worked on his swing, and his mechanics were much better after lessons, but his mind was the real reason for his success. One time, he decided he was going to play in the club's championship flight. We started working weeks ahead of time to prepare him for the tournament. His handicap wasn't good enough to play in that flight, but he wanted to see how he would fare against the best players at the club. We discussed all the scenarios and how to play each hole. We discussed how to handle the bad shots and handle any set-backs that might happen during the round. He had never been under this kind of tournament pressure. He also had all of his buddies telling him how stupid he was to try to play in the championship flight.

Well, the big weekend arrived, and my student, after a pep talk, teed off from the back tees. I intentionally stayed away for the entire round, as I did not want to bother him or possibly see all of our hard work go down the drain. The golf course played tough, and my worry was that a huge number would be posted by my student, who thought his mind was better than that of anyone playing in the tournament. The majority of the players in the field took lessons from me, but my interest really was in this one player's performance. The moment finally came when I saw him

111

in the eighteenth fairway. He hit a good drive and was left with a mid to short iron into the small green guarded by three large bunkers. He hit a good shot and two putts later made par. I was approaching the green to see how the day had gone when he put up his hand to give me a high five and said, "Seventy-two." This was the lowest score he had ever shot, let alone from the back tees. All the work and preparation ended with a two-over-par score on a very difficult golf course.

The story, unfortunately, didn't end with him winning the club championship, but it did leave an impression on me for the rest of my life. If you could think like this student, how good could you become with a good golf swing? Mechanics are very important, and this is a physical game, but my student overcame mechanics that day in the club championship and proved that heart and positive thinking can go a long way!

Tiger Woods's Practice Session at the Open

Last year, my good friend Richard Noon invited me to attend the British Open at Royal Lytham. He called me and told me in his English accent that I must speak to my wife and make this once-in-a-lifetime trip. Usually, if I tell my wife I would like to go on the trip of a lifetime, she asks how many trips of a lifetime are there in a lifetime. She had a point but knew this would be a great trip with one of my best friends. She thought it would be a wonderful experience and told me to go and have a great time.

Richard grew up at Royal Lytham, and his dad is still a member at the prestigious links, which was an added bonus. We booked our flights in January, and Richard starting putting the itinerary together. We played all the great courses near Lytham and even teed it up at Lytham after the Open for two rounds. It really was a trip of a lifetime!

When we arrived in Manchester after a full day's travel, I truly experienced jet lag for the first time. We drove to Richard's parents' house and then headed to the tournament. When we arrived at the gates, it was a unique experience. The English people were fun to be around, and the atmosphere was magical.

Okay, enough about my vacation, let's talk about some useful tips for your golf game. Richard had range passes and handed me my pass. My eyes lit up, and I was thinking, *Are you kidding! I just got off a plane three hours ago, and now I'm walking onto the range at a major championship!* Well, I knew exactly who I was going to watch, and his name was Tiger Woods. I walked to the end of the range where he had started his practice session. I was the closest person to him except for his caddy and watched every shot to see what I could pick up as an instructor. What I noticed after a few minutes of watching him was that he was constantly looking at his yardage book and pulling different clubs. I remembered Hank Haney talking about Tiger having Steve Williams get the pin placements before the round and Tiger hitting those shots on the range before he teed off. Well, I was witnessing this firsthand as Tiger would look through his yardage book and pull clubs to replicate the shot he was going to need for the round.

The first hole at Royal Lytham is a par three, which is unusual for a starting hole, especially for a major championship. Tiger looked at his yardage book for the last time on the range and put it back in his pocket. He pulled what looked like a six iron and proceeded to hit baby cuts. He hit about five shots and then put the club in the bag and left the range to head for the first tee. Tiger had just rehearsed the shots he would be playing for the third round of the Open, and the last shot he hit on the range would be the first shot he would hit on the course.

What a lesson for any player going through a practice session! When Tiger hit his tee shot on the opening hole, it had to have felt like déjà vu. The next time you are going through your warm-up before a big tournament, try this approach. When you leave the range, hit at least three shots that will replicate the shot you will face on the first tee shot. When you get to the tee, it should feel like you've already played the shot.

It was fascinating to watch Tiger warm up. The courses in England are a must play for serious golfers. The fish and chips are the best I've ever had, and England is the only place I've ever been where people asked me where my accent was from. I proudly said, "*Texas*, y'all!"

Tylenol and Advil

One of the most helpless feelings you can get as a parent is when your child is sick. Any of you with children can relate to being up all night when your little ones feel bad. Recently, my youngest son came into our bedroom in the middle of the night complaining that his head hurt. It didn't take long for my wife and me to realize he had a high fever and needed medicine. One rule of thumb we had always heard from our pediatrician was that Advil and Tylenol had to be rotated every four hours to break a fever. We started the Advil, looked at the clock to record what time the medicine had been given, and waited four hours. After we reached the four-hour mark, we went in to check on him. He still had a fever, so we gave him a dose of Tylenol. We repeated this process several times over the next twenty-four hours until his fever was gone.

In golf, I like to use the same formula when a student is struggling to achieve a certain position or a different move during a lesson. I will often prescribe a drill that helps the student feel what I want him to accomplish in his swing. If the student can't do the drill properly, he does not get to hit full shots. Advil becomes the drill, and Tylenol becomes the real swing. My objective is to break the fever in the golf swing.

One example I use a lot is asking the student to take his backswing and hold it at the top until I tell him to swing. You can't fake this drill! This drill makes the student use his upper and lower body rather than hands to control the club. It is always fun to ask the student to take it to the top and hold, but to fail to tell him beforehand that I am going to ask him to swing on my command. The first shot is usually not the best, but after a few times of doing this drill, the student starts to synchronize body and club. Once the student is able to do this, I allow him to hit full shots again. If the student starts hitting bad shots with his full swing, we go back to the drill. Once again, Advil is the drill and Tylenol is the real shot! The student has to go back and forth until he no longer has to take Advil.

There are many times when I use this in teaching. Everyone struggles with something in his game. Identify your fever and ask your pro to prescribe a drill to help you break it. Go back and forth from drill to real shots until you don't have to do the drill anymore. It is a fun way to practice, and there is a consequence attached to every shot. I hope this helps your game and pray that your children always stay healthy.

Watching Your Watch Could Cost You!

About five months ago, I received a call from a doctor who wanted to take lessons. We set an appointment, and when he arrived for his first lesson, he told me what he wanted to get out of his lessons. His main goal was to have fun and to be able to play well enough in front of his friends so he wouldn't embarrass himself. We set up a game plan and got to work on his swing. This doctor was not the most athletic student but really had a passion to get better. This doctor also was unique in his mannerism and could be considered by most to be quite interesting. With all of this said, I looked at our first lesson to be a challenge and an interview for future lessons.

When the lesson was over, he told me he had really enjoyed our time and wanted to book more lessons. In his own words, he told me he was going to be a lesson junkie. This doctor takes a minimum of two lessons per week, now wants to join the club, gives me free medical advice, and has become a friend. This doctor has offered to fly my family up to his home in Montana to ski or play golf and tells everyone to take golf lessons from me.

At the end of our first lesson, I asked him how he had found out about me. He was recommended to me by one of my students who currently plays on the Texas Tech golf team. He also told me he had taken one lesson from a pro at his home club and would never go back. I asked him, out of curiosity, why. He told me the pro had kept looking at his watch during the lesson.

Wax on, Wax off

How many of you have seen *The Karate Kid*? I'm an eighties guy, and the original movie with Ralph Machio is one I've seen a dozen times. When this movie came out, every kid was signing up for karate classes. As a golf instructor, my role is very similar to Mr. Miyagi's. The students have to go through a process, sometimes painful, to achieve what they desire. For all of you reading this who watched the new *Karate Kid* movie, the principles and story line are the same. The karate kid had to learn discipline and technique through a series of drills. Ralph Machio had to sand and paint Mr. Miyagi's fence. When the student finally reached his breaking point and was tired of working, Mr. Miyagi showed him how all the technique could pay off. He threw punches at his student, telling him to wax on, wax off, and the boy was able to block every punch. In the newest movie, one of the drills involved taking a jacket off and putting it back on. All of these drills seemed silly for the characters until they were tested for their real purpose.

Every golf lesson I give ends with some drill the student has to accomplish. All students are different, and rarely do I give the same drill twice in the same week. I analyze the student's flaws and find the best to way to improve them. Once I've established the best route for improvement, I have a drill to work on that helps correct the flaw. Recently, one of my college students was having trouble with compression at impact. I gave the student a compression drill in which the club could go back only to chest height on the backswing and the club had to have forward shaft lean at impact. After the student had hit a few perfect shots with the drill, she asked, "Now can I make a full swing?" You know what I said! She left the lesson with her drill of 1,000 shots with the compression drill before she could return for her next lesson. She sent me a text the next day saying she had already hit 250 balls. This takes tremendous commitment and time, but this is what produces success on the course.

The next time you take a lesson, ask your instructor to give you a specific drill for your flaw. You might hate the process, but at the end of the movie, the karate kid won the fight and got the girl! Get to the range and start. Wax on, wax off!

What I Learned from Stan Utley and Jim Hardy

I had a wonderful opportunity to spend time with two of the best instructors in the game a few months ago. Stan Utley is the hottest short-game teacher in the country, and Jim Hardy is the genius behind the one-plane golf swing. Dr. David Cook wrote a book called *Sacred Journey*, which I highly recommend, and he asked me to bring a few members from Whispering Pines to come to a golf workshop in San Antonio, where Jim Hardy and Stan Utley would be teaching.

As a teacher, this was a chance to learn from the best. I was basically a kid in a candy store, and my entire focus was to soak up as much knowledge from these guys as I could. Jim is one of the most knowledgeable people I have ever met on the golf swing. His basic philosophy is that there are two different swings, which are the one-plane swing and the two-plane swing. I completely agree that all swings can be lumped into one of these two categories. Jim told stories about the tour players he has worked with and kept us entertained every day.

Stan Utley really impressed me because of his humble approach to teaching. He told us it is amazing how smart you become once one of your PGA Tour players wins. I thought this was funny as well as true. When I was at Colonial, one of my students made it through all three stages of PGA Qualifying School to get his card on the PGA Tour. Once the word spread around the club that my student had earned his tour card, my lesson book was packed. My teaching was not any different than it had been the week before my student achieved his dreams, but everyone's perception changed. Stan has a philosophy that has helped many PGA Tour professionals as well as amateurs.

Flying out of San Antonio, I reflected on two incredible days of learning. For me as an instructor, it had been the opportunity of a lifetime. Both of these guys were solid individuals and accomplished much in their careers. I asked each of them if they had desired to become top instructors, and they both told me no. They do what they love, and they do it well. What I took away from the week was that there are different ways to teach. Stan and Jim have their philosophies that are proven. I didn't change my philosophies when I got back to Whispering Pines, but I embraced theirs. There are always opportunities to get better at what you do. Do I teach everyone these techniques? No, but I do use them as situations come up in lessons. The day we stop learning is the day we need to quit doing whatever we are doing. Every day is an opportunity to learn, and I was blessed to have two days of learning with these great instructors.

What I Learned Playing with Clyde Drexler

A few months ago, one of our members invited me to play golf, and one of the people who would make up our foursome was Clyde Drexler. Many of you know Clyde from his years playing with the Houston Rockets, and some non-basketball fans might remember him from the television series *Dancing with the Stars*. I have played with a lot of entertainers and professional athletes over the years, and the one thing they all had in common was their competitiveness. During the round, I asked Clyde what he did when he did not have his best stuff during a basketball game. What he told me was really interesting and can definitely be applied to golf: "When my game wasn't at its best, I tried to play better defense, get on the boards for more rebounds and hustle."

This is one of the many things that made Clyde such a great player. Anyone who plays golf has experienced days when even the best parts of the game were not where you wanted them to be. Some of you reading this might be great putters, but sometimes you can't buy a putt. Some of you hit your driver as straight as Fred Funk but some days can't find a fairway. On the days we struggle, we should take the Clyde Drexler approach. You might not hit your driver down the middle, but your scrambling statistics can be better. When you miss a lot of greens, you can let your short game shine. When you hit in every bunker on the course, you can improve your sand statistics. Look at every round as an opportunity to improve in a different area when you do not have your best stuff. Look at Tiger Woods; he is always at the top or near the top of the leaderboard, even when he is not playing his best. In golf terms, this is called grinding, and players who grind can get the most out of their rounds when it looks bleak.

One of my many philosophies about this crazy game is that you play great golf only about three times a year. Great golf is not about a low score but about all parts of your game firing on all cylinders. Great golf is when the driver through putter works. You can have great scores without hitting all of your shots the way you want. The days when you shoot good scores and don't have your best stuff are the days when you should take Clyde's advice. Next time you are struggling during your round, play better defense, get more rebounds, and hustle. Your attitude and determination will help you shoot a good score when your game is not at its best.

What if All Professional Athletes Were Paid Like Professional Golfers

Can you imagine what Shaq would do if he had to make free throws to keep his job? Can you imagine if every interception that an NFL quarterback threw cost him money? Can you imagine every time a Major League pitcher walked a batter, he would have money taken out of his salary? This sounds absurd, but professional golfers get paid on results. When Tiger Woods was out with his knee surgery, he didn't continue to get a paycheck from all the tour events he was planning on playing. When Mickleson had to cut back his schedule to be with his wife while she was receiving care for cancer, he didn't get a check from the PGA Tour. Now, in contrast, Tony Romo, who I am a huge fan of, missed a large part of the season with an injury and still received a paycheck from Jerry Jones. So why do golfers have different standards than other professional athletes?

We have the NFL possibly not playing football next year because the players and the league can't come to a decision on money. We have multimillionaires wanting more money when they play a game they love. I understand it is a business, but wouldn't it be fun for one season to pay all players on performance?

Let's imagine a running back in the NFL has a $5,000,000 contract for one year. If the running back reaches 1,000 yards, he gets his money. If the running back gets only 900 yards, he receives only $4,000,000 and will continue to lose $1,000,000 for every one hundred yards he loses compared against his starting salary. Let's imagine a Major League batter getting $1,000,000 at the start of the season. For every home run, he gets $100,000 and for every hit, he receives $20,000. I know this is hypothetical because there are sacrifice situations and intentional walks, but let's just pretend for a minute. Now, if the same batter strikes out, he loses $20,000. The better the player, the more money he can make, and the worse he plays, the more money he loses off the base salary. If someone reading this wanted to run the numbers on Peyton Manning, Alex Rodriguez, and Lebron James for a season, I would love to read it.

How about qualifying school for other sports? If you have a really bad year, you have to go back and qualify again for your team. No contracts; just play ball! Wouldn't this solve the majority of the issues of all of these extremely highly paid athletes? Yes, there are other sports, such as tennis, for example, that pay the way golf does, but not team sports. I personally hope there is not a lockout, because I am huge football fan, but it would be interesting to have just one season with this system. I am looking forward to watching the PGA Tour this year with all the new talent, and I will most likely be watching college football, in which students play the game the way it should be played. It is a shame that with all the money athletes make, they ever complain about anything, because the fans will end up paying in the end.

What We Can Learn from Tom Watson's Play in the British Open

Many of you watched this year's British Open and probably felt the same sick feeling that I did after Tom Watson bogeyed the seventy-second hole. I was in South Padre on a family vacation and would not leave my room because I was so amazed at what a fifty-nine-year-old man was about to accomplish at the British Open. Instead of being on the beach, I was glued to a television set, hoping and actually saying a prayer that Watson would play the eighteenth hole in par or better. As we all know, the dream of Tom Watson winning his sixth British Open was lost in a playoff.

Tom Watson played flawless golf all week and was in the headlines of every newspaper around the globe. This would have been one of the greatest sport stories in the history of sports. What other sport could a fifty-nine-year-old have a chance to win against competitors more than forty years younger than him? Let's put this in perspective. Can you imagine Michael Jordan coming back to play in the NBA at age fifty-nine? Can you imagine Roger Staubach playing for the Dallas Cowboys this season? It could never happen! Golf is the only sport where age doesn't stop you from competing. All sports have their limits on longevity, even though Brett Favre is doing his best to keep us confused on why he isn't playing golf instead of playing for a different NFL team every year. We have a ninety-three-year-old man who plays at Whispering Pines at least twice a week. Can you imagine if I took him out to shoot hoops or throw some passes?

The second great thing about Tom Watson almost winning the British Open was the class he showed in defeat. It was painful to watch someone come so close and leave without the Claret Jug. Golf is called a gentlemen's game, and that could not have been more evident when Tom Watson congratulated Stewart Cink on his victory. Tom gave it all he had. He showed us that golf is the greatest of all sports. Tom also showed us that the British Open is the greatest golf tournament because it allows a

Tom Watson or a Todd Hamilton to have a chance against the Tiger Woods of the world. When a golf tournament starts, there are usually only about ten guys who can actually win that week, but that is not the case with the British Open. The Augusta National is so long that the majority of the players do not have a legitimate chance to win. The US Open used to be about the straight hitter, not the bomber, having the best chance to win, but that has changed as they continue to make par fours more than 500 yards in every major . The PGA is not much different from the Masters in the fact that distance is a huge part of the game. Technology has crippled the great traditional golf course of this country, but the links overseas still produce great tournaments without adding 500 extra yards of tee boxes.

I am a sports enthusiast and enjoy many other sports beside golf, but every time I see Terrell Owens whining about not getting enough passes thrown his way or some MLB players arguing with the umpire about a bad call, it makes me proud to be a golf professional. Thank you, Tom, for entertaining us as well as for showing how classy a guy you are!

When Is It Time to Try the Tour?

I recently had a young man tell me he was about to graduate and to try to play professional golf. To be sure, it seems almost all college golfers turn pro after they graduate; however, if you look at the Big 12 golfers who have had success on the tour in the past decade, you could name only a handful. What do all of these guys who don't make it do? Most come to the realization around the age of twenty-eight that the tour might not be right for them. When the guys talk about who they need to beat on the tour, they think about Tiger, Ernie, and Phil. In reality, Fred Funk would beat the majority of the best college players every time.

I feel compelled to write this article because I see a number of young men who have never thought about what they will do if this doesn't work out. I never want to discourage people from chasing their dreams. Dreams are what keep us going. If we are not dreaming, then we are not living. But you should learn to walk before you learn to run. I was fortunate to work at a facility that held a tour event every year. At this facility, tour pros would hit shots in the same places the club pros would hit in their Friday game, but tour pros did it every time. Many times, I would say I could hit a certain shot, and I could, but could I hit it nine out of ten times under pressure? The answer is no. My best day on the golf course was just another day for the tour pros. If I had an eagle putt in a practice round, I would try my best to make it so I could say I made eagle. Tour players, however, pick their eagle attempts and throw them in the bunkers to test the sand.

Lee Trevino once said, "If you have a kid who thinks he is ready to give the tour a shot, take him to ten different golf courses he has never played. The golf courses don't even have to be real hard. If the kid can be under par through ten rounds then he might think about it." Also, Trevino noted that if he didn't shoot sixty-five on his home course, he was upset. Trevino knew every break in the greens and every place to be on the course. Many great young players can break par on their home clubs, but can they do what Lee Trevino says?

128

In closing, don't give up your dreams, and find something to fall back on. The PGA is a great way to go if you love golf and think you might want to be a club pro. There are great players in every section, and there is a tournament every week. The entry fees are affordable, and you are getting a paycheck while working for your club. Don't get into the business if you don't love the game, because club professional jobs are not all about playing. Club professionals service their membership, run businesses, teach, merchandise, and promote the game. You can chase your dreams and still have a career, but never stop dreaming.

When to Watch and When Not to Watch

Recently, my son played in the state golf championship. After watching him play his first round, without saying a word, which was unbelievably hard for me, I noticed something he could improve on in his final round. When I was in college, I played a few rounds with a guy who hit his driver Bubba long with a persimmon wood and a balata golf ball. Now, all of you people under thirty-five reading this article should try hitting with equipment that all of us older guys grew up playing. If you take this challenge, you will find out pretty quickly how good Hogan, Nicklaus, and Nelson were back in the day.

Now, getting back to my son's tournament, I noticed many of the kids in his group were having trouble with different areas of their games. My suggestion to him was to not watch any of his fellow competitors if they were struggling. If one of his fellow competitors was having trouble with short putts, he shouldn't watch. If one of the players had a quick tempo, my son should look down until after he hit the ball. On the contrary, if someone in the group did something very well or something that he could feed off of in his own game, then he should watch.

Well what about that Bubba Long guy? He hit drives back in the late eighties that went 320 yards. He cut the corners of doglegs that I wouldn't even think of trying to cut. I was paired with this guy in one of my last collegiate tournaments, and my coach told me, "Don't try to keep up with this guy!" I knew this would be a challenge, so I decided not to watch any of his swings for the entire round. Once he hit, I would look up and start my routine for my shot or start walking down the fairway if I had already played. This discipline helped me to stay focused on my own game and not try to keep up with Bubba Long. I honestly can't remember if I beat him that day, but I have used this technique and self-discipline in my teaching and tournament rounds ever since that day.

If you were to play with Ben Crenshaw, you should watch every putt. If you were to play with Fred Couples, you should watch his tempo and rhythm all day long. Conversely, if you were playing with someone who has the driver yips or putter yips, you should not watch. Find things in others that you can emulate or that make your round better, and stay away from the things that might make your game worse!

Why Golf Is the Greatest of All Games

Every month, I write articles to various publications about how to play better golf, think better during a round on the golf course, and lower your score. This month, I decided to put in writing the speech that I give to the First Tee kids we teach every week at Whispering Pines Golf Club. First, I want to say it is a privilege to be involved with this program. I and three other golf professionals teach about forty kids every Wednesday and Thursday evening throughout the Houston Independent School District school season. Most of these kids have never played golf and had no intentions of ever playing golf until being exposed to this program. Every Thursday, after we have finished the instruction, I speak to the kids about why golf is the greatest sport ever invented and the reasons they should pursue playing this wonderful game. Here is the typical speech.

Have you ever seen a ninety-year-old man play football, basketball, or baseball? What physical characteristics make a great football player, basketball player, or baseball player? Have you ever gone out and played any of these sports by yourself?

The kids look at me at this point and wonder where I am going with all of this obvious information. I then give them the following information to establish my case.

In golf, we have a ninety-year-old man play Whispering Pines at least once a week. The game of golf has no age limits. Physical characteristics of all the above sports excluding golf require you to be big and strong for football and baseball, and big and tall for basketball. Golf requires no particular physical traits. You can be tall, short, heavy, skinny, and anything in between. Golf does not require you to have someone to play against. You can play alone or play against one hundred people in a tournament. You can also play against players who are more skilled or less skilled than you by incorporating handicaps. In the other sports listed, you really have to play against players who are of the same talent level to have a good match or game.

Last of all, golf is a game of integrity. Have you ever seen Tiger Woods argue with a tour official about a ruling? I think Terrell Owens has done this a few times, along with many of the other high-profile athletes in the other major sports. How about the fights that break out in baseball and basketball from time to time? Have you ever seen a fight break out at a PGA or LPGA Tour? I love all sports and obviously have a reason to believe golf is the greatest sport of all sports. This game has provided me a college scholarship, a wonderful job, many friends, and countless young people whose development as golfers and as human beings I have been fortunate to be part of.

After they have heard my five-minute speech, I ask how many of the kids had thought golf was not much fun before attending First Tee. Almost all of the kids raise their hands and say they had little interest in golf before coming. I then ask how many have changed their minds after First Tee. They almost always all raise their hands. Do I have a great job, or what?

CPSIA information can be obtained at www.ICGtesting.com
Printed in the USA
LVOW12s2111160115

423136LV00002B/3/P